FORWARD

This study is a joint effort of the United States Department of Homeland Security (DHS) in consultation with the National Institute of Standards and Technology (NIST) via the National Cybersecurity Center of Excellence, validated and supplemented by input from industry (vendors, carriers, and service providers), industry organizations, and academic researchers.

DHS is a cabinet department of the United States federal government with responsibilities in public security, roughly comparable to the interior or home ministries of other countries. Its stated missions involve anti-terrorism, border security, immigration and customs, cyber security, and disaster prevention and management.

NIST is a measurement standards laboratory, and a non-regulatory agency of the United States Department of Commerce. Its mission is to promote innovation and industrial competitiveness. NIST's cybersecurity program supports its overall mission to promote U.S. innovation and industrial competitiveness by advancing measurement science, standards, and related technology through research and development in ways that enhance economic security and improve our quality of life.

The need for cybersecurity standards and best practices that address interoperability, usability and privacy has been shown to be critical for the nation. NIST's cybersecurity programs seek to enable greater development and application of practical, innovative security technologies and methodologies that enhance the country's ability to address current and future computer and information security challenges.

The cybersecurity publications produced by NIST cover a wide range of cybersecurity concepts that are carefully designed to work together to produce a holistic approach to cybersecurity primarily for government agencies and constitute the best practices used by industry. This holistic strategy to cybersecurity covers the gamut of security subjects from development of secure encryption standards for communication and storage of information while at rest to how best to recover from a cyber-attack.

The field of computer science is rapidly changing from the basic personal computer to the "Internet of Things". Many of these devices were not designed to be "connected" and very little thought was given to secure them from cyber-attack. Recent events have clearly demonstrated the need to secure everything from web cams to electrical utility grids.

That's where NIST comes in. Just as the National Bureau of Standards set the standard for weights and measures at the beginning of the last century, the 21st century mission for NIST is to set the standard for cybersecurity. NIST gathers the very best minds in industry and government and serves as the central clearing house for information that sets the standard for security for the nation. This publication is only one piece in the mosaic of publications NIST produces but each is a vital key in its own field to the overall cybersecurity strategy that government and industry must adopt in the public interest. All NIST publications are freely available for download over the internet to maximize adoption of the standards.

This publication is an integral part of an overall IT security infrastructure that ensures confidentiality, integrity, and availability of mission critical information. It should be used with other NIST publications to develop a comprehensive approach to managing, satisfying, and verifying an organization's IT security and information assurance requirements.

We here at 4th Watch Books are former government employees so we know how government employees actually use the standards. When a new standard is released, an engineer prints it out, punches holes and puts it in a 3-ring binder. While this is not a big deal for a 5 or 10-page document, many NIST documents are over 100 pages and printing a large document is a time-consuming effort. Unfortunately, reductions in government over the years means that now the engineer himself has to print his own copy (no one has a secretary anymore). So, an engineer that's paid $75 an hour is spending hours simply printing out the tools he needs to do his job. That's time that could be better spent doing engineering.

4th Watch Books prints these documents so engineers can focus on what they were hired to do – engineering. This is important because there are not as many engineers working in government as there used to be, so wasted time on clerical duties is unproductive. As a former senior leader in the government, I always encouraged my subordinates to look for ways to do things better, faster, cheaper. I always asked my staff to focus on the objective and consider the cost/benefit analysis of everything they do. If something can be done better, faster and cheaper, then we would be remiss if we didn't take advantage of the opportunity.

This book is a perfect example of that type of thinking. Rather than spend the limited resources we have at a particular agency to develop cybersecurity solutions, it will always be better, faster and cheaper to embrace a standard that has been fully-developed and totally integrated in the wider scheme of things by the engineers at NIST with the help they receive from industry.

Luis Ayala
Writer and Publisher, 4th Watch Books

Study on Mobile Device Security

April 2017

Science and Technology Directorate

Message from the Under Secretary (Acting) for Science and Technology

April 2017

I am pleased to submit the following report, "Study on Mobile Device Security," which was prepared by the Department of Homeland Security (DHS) in consultation with the National Institute of Standards and Technology (NIST).

This report was prepared pursuant to Section 401 of the *Cybersecurity Act of 2015* (*Consolidated Appropriations Act of 2016*, Div. N, § 401, Pub. L. 114-113, 129 Stat. 2244, 2977-78 [2015]).

Pursuant to congressional requirements, this report is being provided to the following Members of Congress:

      The Honorable Orrin Hatch
      President Pro Tempore of the Senate

      The Honorable Paul Ryan
      Speaker of the House

Should you have any questions, please do not hesitate to contact me.

Sincerely,

Dr. Robert P. Griffin, Jr.
Under Secretary (Acting) for Science and Technology

Executive Summary

Threats to the Government's use of mobile devices are real and exist across all elements of the mobile ecosystem. The enhanced capabilities that mobile devices provide, the ubiquity and diversity of mobile applications, and the typical use of the devices outside the agency's traditional network boundaries requires a security approach that differs substantially from the protections developed for desktop workstations. These are the conclusions of this study, presented to Congress as a joint effort of the Department of Homeland Security (DHS) in consultation with the National Institute of Standards and Technology (NIST) via the National Cybersecurity Center of Excellence, validated and supplemented by input from industry (vendors, carriers, and service providers), industry organizations, and academic researchers.

For the purposes of this study, the term "mobile device" refers to smartphones and tablets running mobile operating systems, as defined in NIST Special Publication 800-53, Revision 4. Mobile phones and the subclass of smartphones represent one of the greatest advances in human communication in history. The world has embraced this technology family as shown by a rapid adoption rate resulting in a global user base, when compared historically to other technologies. According to the Global System for Mobile Alliance (GSMA), the professional body composed of most carriers, mobile network operators and equipment makers, penetration in 2015 reached 4.7 billion unique subscribers globally. By 2020 that number is expected to reach 5.6 billion, meaning that over 70 percent of the world's population will have a mobile subscription.

When viewed against this backdrop, the use of mobile devices by the U.S. Federal Government is an almost insignificant market share. This means that the Government's ability to influence the market cannot be accomplished by purchase power alone, but must instead be achieved via its legislative and regulatory authority. It also means that special care must be taken in the use of these devices because the default level of security is optimized for consumer ease of use, which is not appropriate for Federal employees.

The stakes for government users are high. Government mobile devices—despite being a minor share of the overall market—represent an avenue to attack back-end systems containing data on millions of Americans in addition to sensitive information relevant to government functions. Systems managed by the Department of Defense (DoD), DHS, the Department of the Treasury, the Department of Veterans Affairs, Health and Human Services, the Office of Personnel Management, and others hold significant amounts of sensitive but unclassed information, whose compromise could adversely impact the organization's operations, assets, or individuals. Additionally, databases controlled by these organizations hold tremendous amounts of personally identifiable information (PII) that could potentially be used to compromise citizen financial wellbeing, privacy, or identity.

Threats range from advanced nation state attacks, to organized crime using advanced fraud technologies, to simple theft of mobile phones. The threats to government users of mobile devices include the same threats that target consumers, e.g., call interception and monitoring, user location tracking, attackers seeking financial gain through banking fraud, social engineering, ransomware, identity theft, or theft of the device, services, or any sensitive data. This puts at risk not just mobile device users, but the carriers themselves as well as other infrastructure providers. Government users may be subject to additional threats simply because they are government employees.

Mobile devices are, at their core, consumer devices. While they remain fully functional when running on non-encrypted networks; no notification is provided to the user when operating in this mode. In the United States, there are no regulations requiring carriers to run encryption or provide privacy protections to users on their networks. The caller ID display is unauthenticated and can be made to display any data, including fraudulent information. As early as 1996, members of Congress experienced calls being illegally intercepted, however no technological solution to this problem has been systematically deployed and it remains to this day.

This report categorized the global mobile ecosystem into a threat model organized along clear lines of logical function that also follows industry roles. The threat model's categories consist of:

- Mobile device technology stack, including mobile operating systems and lower level device components
- Mobile applications
- Networks (e.g., cellular, Wi-Fi, Bluetooth) and services provided by network operators
- Device physical access
- Enterprise mobile services and infrastructure, including mobile device management, enterprise mobile app stores and mobile application management

This report addresses each element of the ecosystem with sections providing a detailed summary of the greatest threats in each area as well as current mitigations and defenses. The threat model is examined in detail with further delineation in the newly published draft NIST Interagency Report 8144, *Assessing Threats to Mobile Devices & Infrastructure: The Mobile Threat Catalogue*.

The report has found that mobile device security is improving, and advances have been made by mobile operating systems providers. Mobile device management and enterprise mobility management systems provide managed devices additional scrutiny and security configuration management.

Further improving the landscape are best practices guides issued both by NIST and private industry. This guidance assists enterprises and individuals with instructions on how to configure their mobile devices for security and privacy.

Despite these improvements, many communication paths remain unprotected and leave the overall ecosystem vulnerable to attacks. Significant research remains to be done in this area, as well as hardening of the new fifth generation network protocols, which are currently in early development.

This report identifies threats and documents gaps in available defenses as areas for further research or improvement. Additionally, a framework for modeling mobile threats is presented to assist in the identification of attacker tactics and techniques, which in turn informs areas where current mitigations fall short of protecting mobile devices and information. This report also provides an analysis of emerging threats that are likely to happen based on past trends in crime, the general evolution of cellular network attacks, and advances in academic and public sector security research.

The report lists mobile security best practices collected from NIST, other government agencies, non-government organizations and private industry. It also provides recommendations for assessing some of the risks posed by weaknesses in U.S. networks that appear to be unaddressed by industry. Specifically called out are weaknesses in Signaling System 7 (SS7) and Diameter and the limited response from industry on this highly publicized threat that cannot be solved with changes to end user mobile devices.

Numerous U.S. industry representatives raised concerns with the study group that they have seen little U.S. Government representation on relevant standards bodies. They feel that this puts the U.S. information and communications technology sector at a competitive disadvantage globally.

The study provides recommendations on ways the government can begin to address the identified gaps and weaknesses. These recommendations include programmatic improvements, increased Departmental authorities, adoption of standards and best practices, and areas in need of additional research.

The programmatic improvements, adoption of standards and best practices include the need for increased government participation in standards development, vulnerabilities in mobile networks, and creation of a set of standards and security best practices for mobile application security tailored to government. Additionally, a framework for mobile device security based on existing standards should be adopted. Such a framework would ensure a baseline level of security for Government mobility, while providing the flexibility to address the mission needs, risk profiles, and use cases of Federal Departments and Agencies. This framework would, at minimum, include: mobile application security, enterprise mobility management, mobile device security, and cellular network security.

Adoption of baseline standards and mobile security criteria can provide an increased level of security assurance. Examples include those defined in National Information Assurance Partnership (NIAP) mobile Protection Profiles, the European Union Agency for Network and Information Security, and others. Mobile applications purchased or developed by the Federal Government should be evaluated against the Protection Profile for Application Software and the Requirements for Vetting Mobile Apps. The Government should select mobile devices and enterprise mobility management products that have been evaluated to meet a minimum level of security, e.g., the NIAP Product Compliant List or other Government approved product lists. NIAP approved products must be considered in the context of the environment of use, including appropriate risk analysis and system accreditation requirements. Customers must ensure that the products selected will provide the necessary security functionality for their architecture.

Two gaps in DHS legal authorities to test, verify, or assess and mitigate risks relating to the security of mobile devices within the Federal Government were identified:

- Gap 1: DHS has no legal authority to require mobile carriers to assess risks relating to the security of mobile network infrastructure as it impacts the Government's use of mobile devices.
- Gap 2: While DHS has the authority to evaluate voluntarily provided mobile carrier network information, DHS has no legal authority to compel mobile carrier network owners/operators to provide information to assess the security of these critical communications networks.

DHS proposes several steps to address the identified challenges and to increase security assurance for the Government's use of mobile technology. First, Federal Information Security Modernization Act (FISMA) metrics should be enhanced to focus on securing mobile devices through the Federal Chief Information Officer (CIO) Council's Mobile Technology Tiger Team. The DHS Continuous Diagnostics and Mitigation Program should address the security of mobile devices and applications with capabilities to be at parity with other network devices (e.g., workstations and servers), and the National Protection and Programs Directorate's (NPPD) definition of critical infrastructure should include mobile network infrastructure. DHS Science and Technology (S&T) Homeland Security Advanced Research Projects Agency (HSARPA) Cyber Security Division should continue its work in Mobile Application Security to enable the secure use of mobile applications for Government use. This effort includes continued collaboration with NIAP to automate Mobile Application Security testing. DHS should coordinate mobility adoption with other federal agencies, as inconsistencies across the federal landscape can weaken the best of security practices. Mobile devices inherently present risks to nearby personnel, facilities and systems that may not be intuitively obvious.

Additionally, several new critical research programs should be initiated. Such efforts should include the development of a new DHS applied research and development program to secure mobile network infrastructure and address current and emerging challenges impeding mobile technology. To foster mobile threat information sharing, DHS should develop a new program in advanced defensive security tools and methods for addressing mobile malware and vulnerabilities that spans applied research through operations, including new ways to handle Common Vulnerabilities and Exposures (CVE) generation for mobile. If initiated, DHS should coordinate this program with existing efforts within DoD. Finally, DHS should assess mobile network infrastructure vulnerabilities.

The Federal Government should actively participate in all key mobile security related standards bodies and industry associations, such as the Third Generation Partnership Project and Global System for Mobile Alliance, to better understand risks and help develop consensus-based standards and best practices to represent America's national interests.

NIST should continue to develop its draft *Mobile Threat Catalogue* with additional cooperation from industry and should include emerging threats and defenses and additional risk metrics for mobile threats.

Federal Departments and Agencies should, where needed, develop or strengthen policies and procedures regarding Government use of mobile devices overseas based on threat intelligence and emerging attacker tactics, techniques, and procedures.

The activities described in the preceding paragraphs will improve the security of mobile device use by the U.S. Government as it moves beyond traditional boundaries for information systems to bring citizen services into the field and outside the protections that physical walls, fences, guards, and firewalls provided to enterprise networks and data centers. Compared to the stability and advanced security solutions available for traditional desktops, networks, and servers, the mobile ecosystem continues to evolve, making it more difficult to secure. The sophistication and rapidity of technological advancements in mobility is matched by the evolution of threats against mobile devices, networks, applications, and the mobile technology supply chain overall.

The layered defenses available today should be implemented to ensure delivery of the Government's mission to the American public. Significant advances will need to be made to keep pace with current and emerging threats. These solutions will require collaboration between the public and private sectors to address the needs of the Government for increased mobile security but the solutions will not solely benefit the Government. The Government is only a small percentage of the mobile market. U.S. businesses and citizens could also benefit from improvements in securing the mobile ecosystem. The Department of Homeland Security is responsible for safeguarding the American people, our homeland, and our values. The threats detailed in this paper to cybersecurity in general and mobile security in particular pose serious challenges to the security and resilience of the Nation. DHS needs the proper resources and authorities to address these challenges.

Acknowledgements

The Department of Homeland Security gratefully acknowledges the following organizations for their tireless efforts and commitment to promoting secure mobility in Government, and their direct contributions to the development of this report:

- Department of Defense (DoD)
- Department of Homeland Security Management Directorate, Office of the Chief Information Security Officer (OCISO)
- Department of Homeland Security National Protection and Programs Directorate (NPPD)
- Department of Homeland Security Science and Technology Directorate (S&T)
- General Services Administration (GSA)
- The MITRE Corporation
- National Institute of Standards and Technology (NIST)
- NIST National Cybersecurity Center of Excellence (NCCoE)
- SRI International

In addition, DHS acknowledges and thanks the commercial cellular industry and academic research community for their responses to the "Request for Information: Mobile Threats and Defenses" and participation in one-on-one interviews supporting this study. The study authors sincerely thank the 46 organizations that responded to the RFI, which are listed in Appendix B, and the 13 organizations that participated in one-on-one interviews with the study team; those organizations are listed in Appendix D. This study was completed only through the active participation and support of industry and academia.

Study on Mobile Device Security

Table of Contents

Table of Figures

Table of Tables

I. Legislative Language

This document was compiled pursuant to the legislative language set forth in Section 401 of the *Cybersecurity Act of 2015* (*Consolidated Appropriations Act of 2016*, Div. N, § 401, Pub. L. 114-113, 129 Stat. 2244, 2977-78 [2015]).

Pub. L. 114-113 states:

SEC 401. STUDY ON MOBILE DEVICE SECURITY

(a) IN GENERAL—Not later than 1 year after the date of the enactment of this Act, the Secretary of Homeland Security, in consultation with the Director of the National Institute of Standards and Technology, shall—

    (1) complete a study on threats relating to the security of the mobile devices of the Federal Government; and

    (2) submit an unclassified report to Congress, with a classified annex if necessary, that contains the findings of such study, the recommendations developed under paragraph (3) of subsection (b), the deficiencies, if any, identified under (4) of such subsection, and the plan developed under paragraph (5) of such subsection.

(b) MATTERS STUDIED—In carrying out the study under subsection (a)(1), the Secretary, in consultation with the Director of the National Institute of Standards and Technology, shall—

    (1) assess the evolution of mobile security techniques from a desktop-centric approach, and whether such techniques are adequate to meet current mobile security challenges;

    (2) assess the effect such threats may have on the cybersecurity of the information systems and networks of the Federal Government (except for national security systems or the information systems and networks of the Department of Defense and the intelligence community);

    (3) develop recommendations for addressing such threats based on industry standards and best practices;

    (4) identify any deficiencies in the current authorities of the Secretary that may inhibit the ability of the Secretary to address mobile device security throughout the Federal Government (except for national security systems and the information systems and networks of the Department of Defense and intelligence community); and

    (5) develop a plan for accelerated adoption of secure mobile device technology by the Department of Homeland Security.

(c) INTELLIGENCE COMMUNITY DEFINED—In this section, the term ''intelligence community'' has the meaning given such term in section 3 of the National Security Act of 1947 (50 U.S.C. 3003).

II.   Introduction

This report documents the results of the *Study on Mobile Device Security* required in the *Consolidated Appropriations Act, 2016* Pub. L. 114-113, Division N – Cybersecurity Act of 2015, Title IV, Section 401. The study was conducted during fiscal year 2016 as a collaborative interagency effort led by the Department of Homeland Security's (DHS) Cyber Security Division within the Science and Technology Directorate (S&T) on behalf of the Secretary of DHS, in consultation with the National Institute of Standards and Technology (NIST) via the National Cybersecurity Center of Excellence (NCCoE) on behalf of the Director of NIST. Critical support for the study was provided by the DHS National Protection and Programs Directorate (NPPD), DHS Office of the Chief Information Security Officer (OCISO), General Services Administration (GSA), National Security Agency, and volunteers from other DHS Components and Offices as well as other federal agencies, notably the Department of Defense (DoD).

For the purposes of this study, the term "mobile device" refers to smartphones and tablets running mobile operating systems, as defined in NIST Special Publication 800-53, Revision 4, *Security and Privacy Controls for Federal Information Systems and Organizations*:

> A portable computing device that: (i) has a small form factor such that it can easily be carried by a single individual; (ii) is designed to operate without a physical connection (e.g., wirelessly transmit or receive information); (iii) possesses local, non-removable or removable data storage; and (iv) includes a self-contained power source. Mobile devices may also include voice communication capabilities, on-board sensors that allow the devices to capture information, and/or built-in features for synchronizing local data with remote locations. Examples include smart phones, tablets, and E-readers.

The following were excluded from the study as out of scope:

- Internet of Things
- Supervisory Control and Data Acquisition systems
- Industrial Control Systems
- Customized tablets for dedicated use in a single application, e.g., inventory control or election systems
- Cellular interfaces that are subsystems on other platforms, i.e., automotive Global Positioning System (GPS) or entertainment system
- Devices running mobile operating systems that are fixed in place such as integrated into an automobile, other vehicle, or home appliance

Mobile devices enable anywhere, anytime access to information and services, both for personal use and for Government business. Small, portable, always on, allowing instant Internet access and a diverse set of mobile applications, these computing devices have become indispensable to many people and already are improving workforce productivity. However, their small size, powerful computing capabilities, and the increasing amount of personal and business data accessed by and stored on these devices makes them susceptible to loss or theft and an attractive target for attackers seeking to compromise Government and personal data.

In addition to traditional computing threats such as viruses, worms, malware, and denial of service, mobile devices are more prone to physical attacks and support more complex network interfaces (e.g., cellular, Wi-Fi, Bluetooth, GPS, Near Field Communication [NFC]), exposing more surfaces to attack and posing a unique and evolving set of threats to enterprises. The devices also extend enterprise borders outside of the physical walls, fences, guards and firewalls that previously protected the enterprise against physical attacks. Additionally, they have a full range of sensors not seen in previous computing devices, which enable new types of attacks on the devices as well as the systems they touch.

These threats to mobile security are carried out by threat actors (attackers) who seek to identify and exploit or trigger vulnerabilities in security controls, procedures, architecture, design, coding, or implementation of a system. Threats to Government users of mobile devices include the same threats that target consumers, e.g., call interception and monitoring, user location tracking, attackers seeking financial gain through banking fraud, social engineering, ransomware, identity theft, or theft of the device, services, or any sensitive data. Government users may be subject to additional threats simply because they are Government employees. Furthermore, a threat may target a specific Government agency or type of user—Department/Agency executive, law enforcement official, member of Congress—to steal specific information, embarrass the agency or user, expose data, or

> **THREAT**: *Any circumstance or event with the potential to adversely impact organizational operations and assets, individuals, other organizations, or the Nation through an information system via unauthorized access, destruction, disclosure, or modification of information, and/or denial of service.*
>
> NIST SP 800-30, *Guide for Conducting Risk Assessments*

interrupt/interfere with Government business and missions. Attacks on Government information or systems may target the user, device, software, applications, cellular and wireless networks, mobile services infrastructure, or, frequently, a combination of these essential components of the mobile computing environment. A compromised mobile device may allow remote access to sensitive Government data or any Government or personal data that the user has stored on the device.

The capabilities that mobile devices provide, the ubiquity and diversity of mobile applications, and the typical use of the devices outside the agency's traditional network boundaries requires a security approach that differs substantially from the protections developed for desktop workstations. This report will show that although mobile-specific protections such as isolated enterprise containers, virtual private networks, and the ability to remotely wipe a device mitigate some security challenges, more needs to be done to reduce the risk associated with using these complex mobile information systems.

II.1 Background

Mobile technologies are a foundation of the White House's 2012 Digital Government Strategy that seeks to enable "access to quality digital government information and services anywhere, anytime, on any device."[1] Recognizing that mobile technologies present new and unique security

---

[1] The White House, *Digital Government: Building a 21st Century Platform to Better Serve the American People.* May 23, 2012. Available: https://www.whitehouse.gov/sites/default/files/omb/egov/digital-government/digital-government.html

and privacy challenges, the strategy charged agencies with developing federal standards and best practices to address the security and privacy of digital services. Several interagency groups were established and charged with identifying and addressing common needs and gaps preventing mobile implementations. These groups include:

- Federal Chief Information Officers (CIO) Council's Information Security and Identity Management Committee (ISIMC) Mobile Technology Tiger Team (MTTT)
- ISIMC Identity, Credential and Access Management Subcommittee (ICAMSC)
- MTTT Mobile Application Security Vetting Working Group
- Mobile Services Category Team
- DoD Commercial Mobile Device Working Group

DHS, NIST, GSA, and DoD lead these interagency working groups, which have identified gaps related to policy, standards, and guidance; device management; security assessment and authorization; mobile app development and mobile app vetting; identity management; and interoperability. These groups are actively engaged in solving the Government's mobile security challenges and have developed a mobile security baseline centered on NIST standards, a mobile security reference architecture, security criteria for assessing mobile apps, and guidance on mobile authentication using derived Personal Identity Verification (PIV) and PIV-Interoperability (PIV-I) credentials.

II.2   Study Organizational Leads

DHS S&T and NIST collaborated on the development of this study. Their primary roles in mobile security are described in the following sections.

II.2.1   DHS S&T HSARPA Cyber Security Division Mobile Security Research and Development[2]

Through targeted research and development (R&D), the DHS S&T Mobile Security R&D Program seeks to accelerate the adoption of secure mobile technologies by the Department, the Government, and the global community. To accomplish this vision, the program has established three objectives:

- Partner with DHS Components and federal stakeholders to identify operational requirements and capability gaps.
- Partner with industry to foster innovation.
- Develop secure mobile solutions to enhance the DHS mission.

The program has begun investing in applied R&D to encourage innovative approaches to address mobile security gaps. These initiatives include:

- **Mobile Device Security.** Applied R&D for technologies in: (1) mobile device instrumentation; (2) transactional security methods; (3) device layer protection and mobile security management tools; (4) software-based roots of trust; (5) virtual mobile infrastructure; and (6) mobile app software assurance.

---

[2] https://www.dhs.gov/csd-mobile

4

- **Mobile Application Security.** This new program seeks approaches to provide continuous assurance of security throughout a mobile application's lifecycle by monitoring commercial and federal threat intelligence sources, correlating vulnerabilities across app stores, responsibly sharing threat information, and developing methods to provide actionable information to developers to address threats and vulnerabilities.

II.2.2   NIST National Cybersecurity Center of Excellence

The NIST National Cybersecurity Center of Excellence (NCCoE) is a collaborative hub where industry organizations, Government agencies, and academic institutions work together to address businesses' most pressing cybersecurity issues by developing practical, standards-based solutions using commercially available technologies. Its "Building Blocks" projects address broad technology gaps. The *Mobile Device Security for Enterprises* building block developed an example Mobile Device and Enterprise Mobility Management (EMM) solution that was documented in detail in a Cybersecurity Practice Guide, NIST Special Publication (SP)1800-4, *Mobile Device Security: Cloud & Hybrid Builds*. The guide contains reference architectures; demonstrates implementation of standards-based, commercially available cybersecurity technologies; and helps organizations use technologies to reduce the risk of intrusion via mobile devices. This guidance can be adopted or modified for use by any organization.

In response to comments received on NIST SP 1800-4, the NCCoE's mobile security team also has developed a draft *Mobile Threat Catalogue*[3] and accompanying NIST Interagency Report (NISTIR).[4] The NCCoE also is developing an attack model for mobile as a more concise way to represent the threats in the catalogue. These efforts directly support this study. To develop the catalogue, NCCoE mobile security engineers reviewed mobile security literature to identify major categories of mobile threats and analyzed the threats posed to foundational technologies of the mobile ecosystem. Threats were identified in communication pathways and infrastructure, the mobile supply chain, and at each level of the mobile device technology stack. These threats were placed into threat categories and subcategories with information pertaining to vulnerabilities and specific instances of the threats, alongside applicable mitigation strategies. The draft Mobile Threat Catalogue is undergoing a vetting process by industry and other Government partners.

II.3   Study Methodology

To identify threats to the Government's use of mobile devices and the risk presented to Government information, systems, and networks, it was necessary to define the components of the mobile ecosystem that could be targeted by threats and understand the security features in the standards, protocols, hardware, firmware, and software that enable mobile communications and services throughout the ecosystem.

A subset of threats and threat categories was selected from early versions of the NCCoE's draft *Mobile Threat Catalogue* and agreed to by consensus of the study team. The analysis of threats,

---

[3] C. Brown, et.al., *Mobile Threat Catalogue, Draft*. NIST, 2016. Available: https://pages.nist.gov/mobile-threat-catalogue/
[4] C. Brown, et.al. Assessing Threats to Mobile Devices & Infrastructure, Draft NISTIR 8144. September 2016. Available: https://nccoe.nist.gov/library/nistir-8144-assessing-threats-mobile-devices-infrastructure

vulnerabilities, and defenses against the threats was validated and supplemented by input from industry (vendors, carriers, and service providers), industry organizations, and academic researchers using the following approaches:

- To support the findings and recommendations in this report, a Request for Information (RFI) was issued to the mobile and wireless industry to obtain the latest information on available products and technologies to protect Government information and systems from mobile threats. The RFI was supported by two Industry Days, one held in Washington, D.C. and a second in Menlo Park, California, to answer any questions posed by industry representatives or academic researchers.

- GSA issued the RFI on Mobile Security: Threats and Defenses on July 7, 2016 to obtain input from the mobile and wireless industry and academia (see Appendix A for a synopsis of the RFI). The survey form for the RFI included a set of high-level threats for each threat category. RFI respondents also were asked to fill out the form to indicate which threats their product or technology defends against and whether it provides full or partial mitigation of the threat. Respondents were also asked to provide recommendations on standards and best practices the Government should consider adopting, adapting, or developing to secure its use of mobile devices and services.

- Forty-six organizations responded to the RFI (see Appendix B for a list of respondents). Nineteen respondents also submitted whitepapers further describing their interpretation of the threats and how their products protect against the threats. Nineteen respondents also provided recommendations on mobile security standards and best practices for consideration.

- To obtain industry's view of the overall security of the mobile ecosystem, and how they believed the Federal Government can best improve security of the ecosystem, the study team held one-on-one interviews with experts representing critical elements of the mobile ecosystem. (Quotes from the interviews are called out in several sections of this report and threats and defenses discussed during the interviews are included in the threat assessment. See Appendix C for a list of the one-on-one interview questions and Appendix D for a list of the organizations interviewed).

- The NCCoE hosted a workshop to follow up with select industry segments to highlight threat areas not included in the draft *Mobile Threat Catalogue* and identify new defenses or mitigations. Attendees primarily included those who attended the industry days, responded to the RFI, and participated in one-on-one interviews.

- After analyzing the responses and information provided by industry, the study team documented threats and defenses in each of the threat categories, aligned defenses to the high-level functions of NIST's Cybersecurity Framework, and summarized gaps in available defenses. The analysis cites information from many mobile security commercial entities and researchers when describing mobile threats and vulnerabilities, including footnoted references for additional information. Additionally, the sections include information provided by RFI respondents on defenses against threats. Such identification is neither intended to imply recommendation or endorsement by DHS or the study group, nor is it intended to imply that the entities, services, or equipment are necessarily the best available for the purpose, or that their capabilities have been validated by the

Government.

- Next, the team used the mobile cyber adversary attack model[5] developed by NIST NCCoE to depict methods threat actors might use to carry out an attack. An example is sending a malicious link via email or text message to gain access to the device or to target a vulnerability in the mobile operating system. Using the results of analysis of threats and available defenses, the model was then overlaid with red, green, or yellow, indicating where there are defenses against the threat methods and identifying attacks for which there are limited or no defenses.
- Last, the study team summarized the study's findings and gaps and prioritized threats that require additional action, developed recommendations for secure mobility in Government based on the findings, identified gaps in DHS authorities that may inhibit the ability of the Secretary to address mobile security, and developed the plan for DHS's accelerated adoption of secure mobile technologies.
- The methodology described above—using research, subject matter experts, an RFI, and one-on-one interviews with industry—details our best effort approach to collect and present objective information. Per DHS Information Quality Guidance,[6] this document has been peer reviewed by multiple authors, contributors, DHS and other Federal Departments and Agencies for information objectivity and utility. Any quotes have been formally agreed upon by the respective external organization (e.g. Google, Lookout, etc.).

II.4 Report Structure

The remainder of this report addresses the elements of the legislative language requiring the study on the security of mobile devices. The parenthetical annotations refer to the relevant paragraphs and subparagraphs of the legislation.

Section III. Mobile Ecosystem. Provides context for the report by defining the ecosystem, listing the organizations that develop standards and guidance for the ecosystem, and explains how mobile security techniques evolved from desktop security approaches (b)(1).

Section IV. Mobile Security Threats and Defenses. Addresses the requirements to:

- Identify mobile security threats (a)(1).
- Assess the potential effect of the threats on the Government's information systems and networks (b)(2).
- Explain the threat model developed to portray how threats manifest across the mobile ecosystem and includes an overview of emerging mobile security threats.

Section V. Threat Prioritization, Study Findings, and Gaps. Summarizes the findings of the study, identifies the top threats to mobile security and issues identified by industry during one-on-one interviews, and summarizes gaps in each element of the ecosystem that need to be addressed.

---

[5] Adversarial Tactics, Techniques, and Common Knowledge (ATT&CK™) model and framework developed by the MITRE Corporation for the NCCoE's *Mobile Threat Catalogue*.
[6] https://www.dhs.gov/information-quality-standards.

Section VI. Recommendations for Secure Mobility in Government. Identifies recommended Government and industry standards and best practices as well as any need for policy changes to improve mobile security. This section responds to (b)(3).

Section VII. Gaps in DHS Authorities. Addresses (b)(4).

Section VIII. DHS Next Steps. Provides Congress DHS's proposed initiatives and investment needs to accelerate adoption of secure mobile technology in Government, in response to (b)(5).

III. Mobile Ecosystem

Mobile devices operate within a broader mobile ecosystem that consists of not only the mobile device itself, but also the environment that connects the device to other devices and information systems. Key components of a mobile ecosystem include:

- Mobile device technology stack, including the hardware, the operating system, and embedded mobile device components (e.g., baseband radio, sensors, bootloader, isolated execution environments, Subscriber Identity Module [SIM] card).
- Mobile applications.
- Networks (e.g., cellular, Wi-Fi, Bluetooth, NFC) and services provided by network operators.
- Vendor mobile infrastructure, including mobile app stores and updates and backup services provided by the mobile device vendor or operating-system vendor.
- Enterprise mobile services and infrastructure, including Mobile Device Management (MDM), enterprise mobile app stores, and Mobile Application Management (MAM).

All these individual ecosystem components must be considered when assessing the security of mobile devices. Figure 1 provides an overview of the mobile ecosystem.

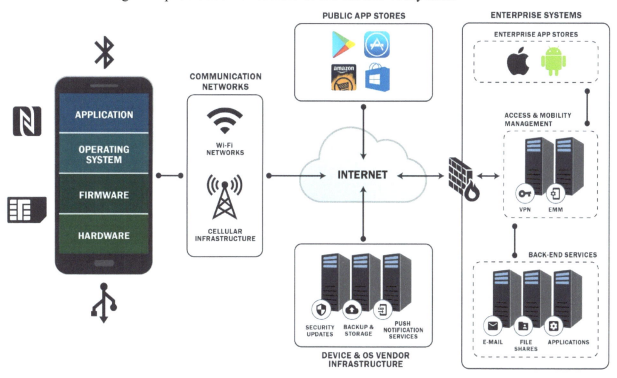

Figure 1. Mobile Ecosystem

The vast size of the consumer market (4.7 billion unique users[7]) and nongovernment enterprise market for mobile devices suggests limitations in the Government's ability to influence the security approaches taken by mobile device ecosystem vendors. The Government's influence has

---

[7] GSMA, The Mobile Economy 2016. http://www.gsma.com/mobileeconomy/

9

eroded. The stakes for Government users are high, however. Government mobile devices—despite being a minor share of the overall market—represent an avenue to attack enterprise systems containing data on millions of Americans in addition to the sensitive information relevant to Government functions. Databases controlled by the Department of Defense, DHS, Department of the Treasury, Department of Veterans Affairs, Health and Human Services, the Office of Personnel Management, and other Government agencies hold tremendous amounts of personally identifiable information (PII) that could potentially be used to compromise the financial wellbeing, privacy, or identity of individuals.

As described in Section IV.2.1, mobile device vendors have taken novel approaches to security architectures beyond the traditional approaches of desktop personal computers (PCs). Additionally, the National Information Assurance Partnership (NIAP) has had great success collaborating with the mobile industry through its Mobility Technical Community to develop technology-specific security requirements for mobile devices and mobile device management solutions. Numerous vendors, including Apple, Boeing, LG, Microsoft, MobileIron, and Samsung have successfully taken mobility products through Common Criteria evaluations against these requirements. For more information concerning NIAP and the security requirements documentation, refer to Section III.2.

Security requires integrity from individual components and also how they work together as an integrated system.

Qualcomm

III.1 Approach to Mobile Security

Mobile devices on the market today are some of the most complex and capable computing devices ever created. Although many can now match the capabilities of desktops and are being marketed as desktop replacements, they have features and capabilities not available to any desktop. They also sit in the broader mobile ecosystem giving them significantly more exposure. This means they share many of the same security threats as traditional desktop and laptop computers and are also exposed to more threats brought about by their mobility, complexity, and additional sensors. The impact of many of these threats can be magnified by the unique attributes of mobile devices.

As depicted in Figure 2, these unique attributes include their almost always powered-on state, ubiquitous network connectivity, multiple radio interfaces (cellular, Wi-Fi, NFC, Bluetooth), and inclusion of a wide variety of sensors including biometric, GPS, compass, gyroscope, barometer, camera, and microphone array. These properties mean a desktop approach to security is not sufficient. For instance, no desktop PC could eavesdrop on a conversation using its gyroscopic sensor[8] because no desktop has ever been equipped with one, however, that is but one new threat of hundreds in the mobile device landscape. The full breadth and depth of these threats is examined in the NIST Interagency Report (NISTIR) 8144, *Assessing Threats to Mobile Devices & Infrastructure: The Mobile Threat Catalogue* appendix.

---

[8] Y. Michaevsky and D. Bone. Gyrophone: Recognizing Speech from Gyroscope Signals. 23rd USENIX Security Symposium. August 20-22, 2014.

CELLULAR

Used for voice, text, and data services provided by cell radio network carriers

BLUETOOTH TECHNOLOGY

Personal area networking used for file sharing and linking peripheral devices

NEAR-FIELD COMMUNICATION (NFC)

Used for low data rate transfers, smart card emulation, and reading RFID tags

SUBSCRIBER IDENTITY MODULE (SIM)

Removable hardware token providing data storage and cellular access

BIOMETRIC AUTHENTICATION

Used to scan fingerprints to unlock the device

Wi-Fi

Local area networking used for access to connected resources of the Internet

SECURE DIGITAL (SD) CARD

Used for additional storage capacity or transferring data between devices

GLOBAL POSITIONING SYSTEM (GPS)

Use of orbiting satellites to determine the geographic location of the device

POWER SYNCHRONIZATION CABLE

Wired connection used for charging and exchanging data with a computer

ENVIRONMENTAL SENSORS

Used for a wide range of input including precise navigation, game controls, and screen brightness

Figure 2. Mobile Device Interfaces

Mobile device isolation capabilities provide security benefits, but also mean approaches beyond the traditional endpoint protection techniques used on enterprise desktop PCs must be adopted to monitor the state of mobile devices against emerging threats. For example, on desktop PCs, third-party host-based security products (e.g., antivirus software or endpoint protection) are typically used in enterprise environments to detect and respond to threats. These products run at a highly privileged level, enabling them to deeply inspect system state and identify threats that network-based monitoring alone cannot identify. However, on mobile devices, the isolation technologies applied to mobile applications severely limits the capabilities of third-party security applications compared to what is possible in the PC environment. In general, third-party security applications are limited to the interfaces provided by the operating system to gather system state information.

Similarly, enterprise environments typically use network-based intrusion detection systems (IDS) to monitor network traffic for malicious activity to or from enterprise computing systems. These techniques are less effective on mobile devices because mobile devices are only sometimes connected to the enterprise network, while at other times they are connected to cellular networks or public Wi-Fi networks that are not monitored by the enterprise. Additionally, mobile operating systems typically treat the network as untrusted, encrypting most or all network data communications, thereby limiting the potential visibility of network-based IDS into malicious activity.

Strong authentication should be leveraged for mobile devices, as it is for traditional desktop and on premise devices. However, the desktop centric approaches to strong authentication are not designed to be easily interoperable with mobile form factors. New approaches are needed to leverage the unique capabilities of the mobile device to capture data from the device user that uniquely identifies and validates the user's identity. To this end, there is active research and development that seeks to use the data being captured by a mobile device's sensors to securely and continuously authenticate a device user. Data points compiled from device components such as the motion sensor/accelerometer, gyroscope, GPS, force sensor, capacitive sensor, and camera can be used to uniquely identify a user via analysis of patterns captured by the device sensors. As this technology matures it has the potential to offer users a less obtrusive and stronger method by which to securely authenticate a user to their device and the data it contains. The sensor data could also be used to make decisions about a user's ability to access specific data types. Data access control decisions could be made at a much more granular level thereby providing increased control to sensitive information types based on proven geographical and temporal data points.

The isolation capabilities of mobile operating systems are designed to provide protection against malicious behavior by controlling the allowed interactions between users and applications, and between each application and the underlying device components. The specific details vary between mobile platforms, but in general, mobile applications must obtain consent from the device user before accessing sensitive device capabilities (e.g., the device's geolocation functionality) or accessing sensitive device information repositories (e.g., the device's contacts database) but not most a device's sensors. Increasingly, mobile applications cannot directly access data stored by other applications without authorization. These security architecture properties provide a degree of protection, however, compared to desktops, security for mobile devices is immature and gaps remain.

III.2 Standards and Best Practices Overview

The following is an overview of several key Standards Development Organizations (SDOs) and the technical and security standards and protocols they develop for the mobile ecosystem. The development, review, and dissemination of technical and operational standards and best practices are critical to maintaining interoperability and establishing minimum standards of quality within a given technology area. These standards often are imposed by Government fiat, but various standards bodies consisting of manufacturers, academia, and nonprofit organizations have been formed to develop consensus standards independent of Government mandates. Many standards bodies increasingly seek to include basic security measures—such as encryption, authentication, and integrity checking—as core features of their standards and protocols.

Bluetooth Special Interest Group (SIG). The Bluetooth SIG develops the standards and specifications for the Bluetooth wireless communications protocol. The Bluetooth specifications include features designed to provide a high quality of service as well as improved security. These include frequency-hopping, which may reduce interference with other devices and make it more difficult for eavesdroppers to intercept data, integrated support for strong encryption, and man-in-the-middle protections against eavesdropping and data modification.

Global System for Mobile (GSM) Alliance (GSMA). GSMA is the professional body funded by and run for the benefit of most the world's mobile network operators along with handset and network equipment manufacturers. It provides best practices for the secure operation of networks, application coding, SIM distribution and operation, and many other aspects of the mobile device ecosystem. GSMA also runs the largest two conferences in the world focused solely on the mobile ecosystem: the GSMA World Congress held in Barcelona and the GSMA World Congress Asia held in Shanghai.

GlobalPlatform. GlobalPlatform is a standards body similar to the Trusted Computing Group (TCG) in that its primary focus is developing security standards and technologies. Its purview is narrower than TCG's, however, in that its area of concern is the design and development of secure chip technology. GlobalPlatform also is involved in the definition of use cases and exploration of the applicability of secure chip technology to different sectors of the market. Among GlobalPlatform's key technologies are secure chips known as "secure elements" that host and protect applications and data and perform cryptographic operations. Secure elements can be found in smart cards, chip-enabled credit and debit cards, and identification cards. They are also found in many mobile devices. The secure chips can be used to store cryptographic keys, facilitate encryption and decryption, derive cryptographic keys, facilitate software integrity checking, and support secure boot operations. Secure elements are conceptually similar to Trusted Platform Modules (TPM); however, secure elements are often implemented in more lightweight form factors that are better suited to use cases that need small, energy-efficient solutions.

Institute of Electrical and Electronics Engineers (IEEE). IEEE is comprised of practitioners from technical fields ranging from electrical and electronics engineers to computer scientists, software engineers, medical professionals, and scientists from around the world. Several technical standards developed by IEEE have direct bearing on the mobile ecosystem. There is significant overlap in membership between IEEE and several of the other standards bodies referenced in this document. The symbiotic relationship between IEEE and other standards organizations means that IEEE standards are adopted or incorporated in products, technologies, and standards developed by these bodies, and these bodies develop and propose standards that eventually become official IEEE standards. For example, the 802.11 series of Wireless LAN standards were developed and published by IEEE, and eventually branded Wi-Fi® and championed by the Wi-Fi Alliance® consortium of companies. The Wi-Fi Alliance in turn contributes standards to—and develops products and technologies based upon—802.11.

International Organization for Standardization (ISO). ISO is comprised of the national SDOs of most of the world's nations. ISO generates a wide variety of standards that touch on many aspects of economic and industrial activity. The ISO 27000 family of standards provides requirements for data protection, with ISO 27001 providing requirements for information security management systems. Several of the most prominent vendors and service providers in the mobile ecosystem have achieved ISO 27001 certification. This certification provides their customers assurance that these organizations have integrated strong, internationally recognized, security best practices for their people, processes and information technology systems.

Internet Engineering Task Force (IETF). The Internet Society's IETF has developed and released several security standards. Among the most well-known is Transport Layer Security (TLS), formerly known as Secure Sockets Layer (SSL). TLS is important for the mobile ecosystem since it is the most common standard used to secure connections between mobile devices and Internet-connected systems. It is also used to secure other components of the mobile ecosystem, including the administrative interfaces for network devices, MDM servers, and other relevant enterprise systems. Internet Protocol Security (IPsec), which provides secure end-to-end connections, especially in the context of Virtual Private Networks (VPNs), also is used to administer the systems used to manage mobile devices. IPsec may also be used to provide secure connections between mobile devices and the enterprise networks to which the mobile devices connect.

National Information Assurance Partnership (NIAP). NIAP is a U.S. Government program to collaboratively develop standards-based Protection Profiles, oversee evaluations of commercial information technology (IT) products for use in National Security Systems (NSS), and represent the U.S. in the international Common Criteria Recognition Arrangement (CCRA).

Protection Profiles (PPs) define implementation-independent security requirements and test activities for a specific technology to enable achievable, repeatable, and testable product evaluations. PPs are used to validate the security functionality of products during Common Criteria (CC) evaluations, but may also be used for other accreditation or validation activities that do not involve CC certification.

The security objectives covered by NIAP PPs include protected communication, protected storage, mobile device configuration, authorization and authentication, and mobile device integrity. NIAP currently manages a suite of PPs that apply to mobile technologies, including the Protection Profile for Mobile Device Fundamentals, the Protection Profile for Mobile Device Management, and the Protection Profile for Application Software. As of September 2016, the following mobility-related Protection Profiles are available:

- Protection Profile for Mobile Device Fundamentals Version 3.0
- Protection Profile for Application Software Version 1.2 and Requirements for Vetting Mobile Apps from the Protection Profile for Application Software
- Application Software Extended Package for Email Clients v2.0
- Application Software Extended Package for Web Browsers v2.0
- Extended Package for Software File Encryption Version 1.0
- Protection Profile for VOIP Applications Version 1.3
- Protection Profile for IPsec Virtual Private Network (VPN) Clients Version 1.4
- Protection Profile for Mobile Device Management Version 2.0
- Extended Package for Mobile Device Management Agents Version 2.0

PPs are updated regularly to keep pace with the evolving threat landscape and to reflect changes in product capabilities and features. New PPs are developed to address new and emerging technologies of interest to U.S. Government customers.

Near Field Communication Forum (NFC Forum). NFC is a set of communication protocols developed by the NFC Forum. It is designed to enable data exchanges at extremely close ranges (less than 3 inches). The integration of NFC technology into mobile devices is increasing because it enables an expanding number of capabilities. For example, beyond paying for goods and services, NFC use cases have been developed to meet needs as diverse as exchanging and synchronizing data, replacing key cards at hotels and other facilities, tracking items and managing inventory, and tracking medications in health care. NFC is designed such that security can be integrated at multiple points in the protocol stack. However, researchers have demonstrated a variety of attacks that challenge some of these assertions, including the premise that NFC's transmission range only extends to a few inches.

NIST Information Technology Laboratory (ITL). The ITL is one of seven research laboratories within NIST that develop and deploy standards, tests, and metrics to make information systems more secure, usable, interoperable, and reliable. ITL's responsibilities include the development of management, administrative, technical, and physical standards and guidelines for the cost-effective security and privacy of other than national security information in federal information systems. OMB Circular A-130[9] requires agencies to follow NIST standards and policies, specifically stating: "For non-national security programs and information systems, agencies must follow NIST guidelines unless otherwise stated by OMB. Federal Information Processing Standards (FIPS) are mandatory." NIST's Cryptographic Algorithm Validation Program (CAVP) tests that cryptographic algorithms deemed acceptable for use in federal systems are correctly implemented. A corresponding program—the Cryptographic Module Validation Program (CMVP)—tests that cryptographic modules are correctly implemented per NIST FIPS. Several FIPS-mandated algorithms are commonly used to provide secure communications within the mobile ecosystem. For example, the Advanced Encryption Standard (AES) algorithm is a NIST standard cryptographic algorithm commonly used to encrypt data sent using TLS and IPsec or to protect data stored on a disk, while algorithms specified by NIST's Secure Hash Standard are used to ensure data integrity.

Third Generation Partnership Project (3GPP). 3GPP is an international SDO created to develop and manage telecommunications standards. Although initially created to develop the third-generation Universal Mobile Telecommunications System (UMTS) set of standards, it has since developed the Long Term Evolution (LTE) standard as well as derivatives such as LTE Advanced and over-the-horizon, fifth-generation (5G) standards. Despite the 3GPP's close attention to security, several LTE-related vulnerabilities have been discovered and published. These vulnerabilities affect even the most current versions of the LTE standards and potentially allow illicit eavesdropping, denial of service, data and service theft, and other attacks.[10]

Trusted Computing Group (TCG). The TCG is a standards body composed of representatives from industry, academia, Government organizations, and nonprofit organizations from around the world. There are several TCG working groups involved in technical areas as diverse as cloud computing, mobility, network communications, virtualization, and secure chip technologies.[11] The TCG is the originator of the TPM standards and protocols for the design and use of secure hardware modules that serve as the root of trust on many kinds of devices. Among the capabilities provided by hardware modules that comply with the TPM specifications are the ability to derive and securely store cryptographic keys, mediate authentication requests, perform a variety of cryptographic operations, store information about the state of machines in which they are embedded, and verify that the machines are allowed to operate only if they maintain a trusted state. TPMs are installed in most modern laptops, some servers, and some mobile devices.

Universal Serial Bus (USB) Implementers Forum. The companies that invented the USB technology created a standards body, the USB Implementers Forum (USB-IF), to continue oversight and development of the specification and to promote USB. The USB-IF's responsibilities include the development of standards for testing device compliance, arranging various developer and compliance conferences and workshops, and marketing USB technology and standards.[12] From a security perspective, USB presents a threat because of vulnerabilities

---

[9] https://www.whitehouse.gov/sites/default/files/omb/assets/OMB/circulars/a130/a130revised.pdf
[10] 4G LTE Security for Mobile Network Operators. Cyber Security and Information Systems Information Analysis Center. https://www.csiac.org/journal-article/4g-lte-security-for-mobile-network-operators/. Accessed 8/22/2016.
[11] "About the Trusted Computing Group." Trusted Computing Group. http://www.trustedcomputinggroup.org/about/. Accessed 8/23/2016.
[12] "About USB Implementers Forum, Inc." USB Implementers Forum. http://www.usb.org/about. Accessed 8/23/2016.

that may be inherent to the standard or the specific USB implementations, and because USB cables provide physical access to a mobile device and its data.

Wi-Fi Alliance. The Wi-Fi Alliance is a global nonprofit consortium of companies established in the late 1990s to develop, implement, and evangelize the standards and protocols that collectively comprise Wi-Fi. Since its introduction, a number of serious Wi-Fi-related vulnerabilities have been discovered and mitigated, ranging from the ability to deny network service to the ability to intercept and/or derive the encryption keys used to protect Wi-Fi traffic. The Wi-Fi Alliance has created a dedicated security working group to develop and certify security standards for current and emerging Wi-Fi technologies. Among these standards are Wi-Fi Protected Access version 2 (WPA2) and Wi-Fi Protected Setup (WPS).

III.3 Cybersecurity Strategy and Implementation Plan

The Cybersecurity Strategy and Implementation Plan (CSIP) (Office of Management and Budget [OMB] M-16-04) directs a series of actions to improve capabilities to identify and detect vulnerabilities and threats, strengthen protections of Government assets/information, and develop enhanced response/recovery capabilities to allow readiness/resilience when incidents occur. The CSIP identified key actions to be implemented by Federal Agencies, namely:

1. Agencies will continue to identify high-value assets (HVAs) and critical systems to understand their potential impact from a cyber incident and ensure robust physical and cybersecurity protections are in place.
2. DHS will accelerate the deployment of Continuous Diagnostics and Mitigation (CDM) and EINSTEIN[13] capabilities to all participating Federal agencies to enhance detection of cyber vulnerabilities and protection from cyber threats. DHS is extending capabilities of EINSTEIN's third phase, called EINSTEIN 3 Accelerated, to include behavioral analytics.
3. All Agencies will improve the identity and access management of user accounts on Federal information systems to drastically reduce vulnerabilities and successful intrusions.
4. OMB, in coordination with the National Security Council (NSC) and DHS, will issue incident response best practices for use by Federal agencies. CSIP directs agencies to patch all vulnerabilities immediately or, at minimum, within 30 days of patch release.

Of critical importance for addressing mobile security threats are items (2) and (3), which are specific to the inclusion of mobile devices within the scope of the CDM program.

---

[13] EINSTEIN serves two key roles in federal government cybersecurity. First, EINSTEIN detects and blocks cyber-attacks from compromising federal agencies. Second, EINSTEIN provides DHS with the situational awareness to use threat information detected in one agency to protect the rest of the government and to help the private sector protect itself.

IV. Mobile Security Threats and Defenses

The functionality provided by mobile devices has evolved over the past two and a half decades and continues to advance. When first introduced, mobile phones were basic cellular phones designed to make telephone calls and send text messages. Although carriers were targeted by various criminal fraud schemes, users and their data were rarely the target of criminals. Once modern mobile operating systems (OS) were introduced, the threat landscape changed drastically as users began trusting these devices with large quantities of sensitive personal information and mobile network operators integrated data and voice networks. Commercial enterprises also started allowing employees to use mobile devices and applications to access enterprise email, contacts, and calendar functionality.

IV.1 Mobile Security Threats and Threat Categories

This study examined five primary components of the mobile ecosystem and their associated attack surface: the mobile device technology stack, mobile applications, mobile network protocols and services, physical access to the device, and enterprise mobile infrastructure. These five threat categories and the types of threats analyzed for this study were selected to provide Congress a broad view of the threats to the Government's use of mobile devices and the major elements of the mobile ecosystem. While these threats are grouped into categories, it is noted that threats seldom impact only one element of the ecosystem. Therefore, defenses must cover the entire threat surface, not just a single category.

Although everyone is using mobile, a sense of urgency in securing the mobile environment is lacking.

Lookout

Attackers can gain access to information and systems or deny services in numerous ways. Security defenses are put in place to protect mobile users, data, systems, networks, and services from attacks. Table 1 represents a high-level summary of the types of threats to the mobile ecosystem. These threats compromise the confidentiality, integrity, and availability of Government information and systems, and pose risk to the safety and privacy of users. The threats defined in the following sections fall into one or more of these areas.

Table 1. Basic Types of Mobile Threats

Threat	Definition	Examples
Denial of Service	Deny or degrade service to users.	Jamming of wireless communications, overloading networks with bogus traffic, ransomware, theft of mobile device or mobile services.
Geolocation	Physical tracking of user.	Passively or actively obtaining accurate three-dimensional coordinates of target, possibly including speed and direction.
Information Disclosure	Unauthorized access to information or services.	Interception of data in transit, leakage or exfiltration of user, app, or enterprise data, tracking of user location, eavesdropping on voice or data communications, surreptitiously activating the phone's microphone or camera to spy on the user.

Threat	Definition	Examples
Denial of Service	Deny or degrade service to users.	Jamming of wireless communications, overloading networks with bogus traffic, ransomware, theft of mobile device or mobile services.
Geolocation	Physical tracking of user.	Passively or actively obtaining accurate three-dimensional coordinates of target, possibly including speed and direction.
Information Disclosure	Unauthorized access to information or services.	Interception of data in transit, leakage or exfiltration of user, app, or enterprise data, tracking of user location, eavesdropping on voice or data communications, surreptitiously activating the phone's microphone or camera to spy on the user.
Spoofing	Impersonating something or someone.	Email or SMS message pretending to be from boss or colleague (social engineering); fraudulent Wi-Fi access point or cellular base station mimicking a legitimate one.
Tampering	Modifying data, software, firmware, or hardware without authorization.	Modifying data in transit, inserting tampered hardware or software into supply chain, repackaging legitimate app with malware, modifying network or device configuration (e.g., jailbreaking or rooting a phone).

Figure 3 depicts some of the threats in each threat category; these threats are described in Section IV.1.2 through IV.1.6.

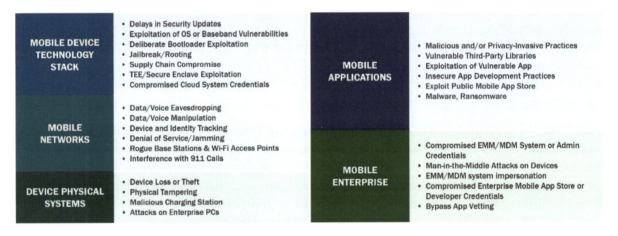

Figure 3. Mobile Security Threats by Threat Category

The following sections describe threats, vulnerabilities, and available defenses that mitigate the threats. If no effective mitigation has been identified for a threat or class of threats, it is called out as a gap. In the concluding section of each threat category, the defenses are summarized in a table that maps the defense to the security control functions of the NIST Cybersecurity Framework[14] (identify, protect, detect, respond, recover), followed by a section listing gaps in mitigations. To show how threats occur across the elements of the mobile ecosystem, the summary is followed by a framework for modeling mobile security threats and depicting gaps in defenses. The concluding section discusses emerging threats to the mobile ecosystem.

---

[14] NIST, Framework for Improving Critical Infrastructure Security. Version 1.0. February 12, 2014. https://www.nist.gov/sites/default/files/documents/cyberframework/cybersecurity-framework-021214.pdf

The descriptions in the following sections generally use the Android and iOS platforms when providing examples. A Gartner report shows these platforms combined held a 99.1 percent global market share of mobile device sales in the second quarter of 2016.[15] Similar principles apply to platforms such as Windows and BlackBerry. These sections also cite information from many mobile security commercial entities and researchers when describing mobile threats and vulnerabilities, with footnoted references for additional information. Additionally, the sections include information provided by RFI respondents on defenses against threats. Such identification is neither intended to imply recommendation or endorsement by DHS or the study group, nor is it intended to imply that the entities, services, or equipment are necessarily the best available for the purpose, or that their capabilities have been validated by the Government. Some of the solutions described by RFI respondents are offered by companies in foreign countries.

IV.2 Mobile Device Technology Stack

Figure 4 shows the multiple technology layers of a mobile device, from the hardware itself through the firmware and mobile operating system to the mobile applications and data.

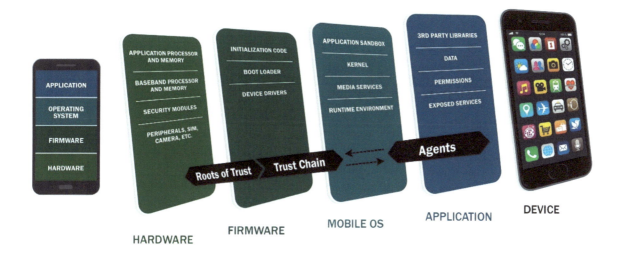

Vulnerabilities in any of these components may be targeted by threats.

Figure 4. Mobile Device Technology Stack

IV.2.1 Mobile Operating System

The security architecture of mobile operating systems serves an important role in protecting the mobile device from exploitation. The application isolation capabilities of mobile operating systems are designed to provide protection against malicious behavior by controlling the allowed interactions between applications and between each application and underlying device components. In some mobile operating systems, applications cannot access data stored by other

---

[15] http://www.gartner.com/newsroom/id/3415117

applications and applications are restricted from interfering with the behavior of another application. Applications must obtain user consent to access device capabilities such as the microphone, camera, or GPS or to access sensitive information repositories such as contact lists. The presence of application isolation generally means that even if a malicious or vulnerable application is installed onto a mobile device, it cannot steal or otherwise tamper with the data of another application.

The application package management capabilities of mobile operating systems provide control over what applications can be installed on mobile devices. The mobile operating system ensures that applications and their updates are only installed from authorized sources (unless the device is configured otherwise).

IV.2.1.1 Threats

Exploitation of mobile operating system vulnerabilities can provide an attacker the ability to bypass the important security protections provided by the operating system, including the application isolation and package management capabilities, resulting in impacts including attacker access to sensitive enterprise data. Just as with any software, vulnerabilities are constantly discovered in mobile operating systems. Typically, on notification of a vulnerability, mobile operating system vendors fix the issue and the fix (often referred to as a patch) is also included in a software update.

Most Android devices historically have been left unpatched for long periods against published vulnerabilities, leaving the devices at risk of exploitation.[16] Android has a complex patch lifecycle involving multiple entities including Google as the operating system vendor, the device vendor, and the wireless carrier, which has caused delays in issuing software updates. In some cases, the device may no longer be supported by its vendor or wireless carrier, resulting in software updates for that device never being issued. Mobile security firm Lookout provided an explanation of the Android security update challenge and its impact in a 2011 blog post[17] and accompanying Black Hat USA 2011 presentation. An open-source Android application—the Android Vulnerability Test Suite (VTS)[18]—developed by NowSecure, runs tests on the mobile device to help users assess their own device's susceptibility to a number of publicly known vulnerabilities. In its 2016 mobile security report, NowSecure reported that 82 percent of Android devices that ran its VTS app and chose to report the results were susceptible to at least one vulnerability.

> *Our major objective for mobile security is to provide a broad and comprehensive set of protections, widely available, at no cost. Security is something everybody should have by default, and it should be free.*
>
> Google Inc.

---

[16] https://developer.android.com/about/dashboards/index.html
[17] https://blog.lookout.com/blog/2011/08/04/inside-the-android-security-patch-lifecycle/
[18] https://github.com/AndroidVTS/android-vts

The Federal Trade Commission (FTC)[19] and Federal Communications Commission (FCC)[20] announced in May 2016 efforts to assess the mobile device security update process. Not only do new operating system versions bring patches against specific vulnerabilities, new versions often bring security architecture improvements that provide resilience against potential vulnerabilities or weaknesses that have not yet been discovered.

Recent indications reveal that the Android security patch lifecycle is improving. Google has begun including an "Android security patch level" indicator on Android devices. It allows users and enterprises to quickly assess the security state of their Android devices. On Google's Nexus and Pixel line of Android devices—devices that are designed or manufactured and directly controlled by Google rather than a third-party Android device vendor—security patches have been distributed quickly and Google has committed to provide patches for a set period (i.e., Nexus devices and Pixel phones will get Android version updates for at least two years from when the device became available on the Google Store; Android One partners have committed to providing software updates for at least 18 months after the phone's launch).[21] Other Android device vendors such as BlackBerry[22] have committed to providing security patches in a timely manner. A May 2016 *Bloomberg* article[23] details efforts by Google to step up pressure on vendors and carriers. Nick Kralevich of Google's Android Security Team provided data indicating that the current flagship Android devices from major device vendors are now receiving patches in a timely manner. [24]

Mobile operating system vendors have invested in security architecture improvements designed to either prevent or limit the impact of exploitation of vulnerabilities. Google's Kralevich also discussed in his Black Hat USA 2016 presentation efforts to not just patch individual vulnerabilities on discovery, but also seek to identify root causes and architecturally eliminate exploitation of entire classes of vulnerabilities.[25] For example, based on code contributions from the NSA's Trusted Systems Research Group and others, Android now uses Security-Enhanced Linux (SELinux) to strengthen its security architecture.[26] Some individual Android vendors have incorporated their own security features in addition to what Google provides. For example, many of Samsung's Android devices feature additional security capabilities such as their Real-time Kernel Protection (RKP) feature and TrustZone-based Integrity Measurement Architecture (TIMA) to detect and respond to indications of device compromise. However, these technologies are not foolproof, as demonstrated by work by the Israel-based Viral Security Group, which wrote a whitepaper describing techniques to bypass Samsung's RKP.[27] Apple likewise has an excellent track record of continual improvements to iOS security architecture. Many of the elements of the iOS security architecture are documented in Apple's publicly available iOS Security Guide white paper.[28] Ivan Krstic, head of Apple Security Engineering and Architecture,

---

[19] https://www.ftc.gov/news-events/press-releases/2016/05/ftc-study-mobile-device-industrys-security-update-practices
[20] https://www.fcc.gov/document/fcc-launches-inquiry-mobile-device-security-updates
[21] https://support.google.com/nexus/answer/4457705#nexus_devices
[22] http://blogs.blackberry.com/2015/11/managing-android-security-patching-for-priv/
[23] http://www.bloomberg.com/news/articles/2016-05-25/google-steps-up-pressure-on-partners-tardy-in-updating-android
[24] https://www.blackhat.com/us-16/briefings.html#nick-kralevich
[25] Ibid.
[26] https://source.android.com/security/selinux/index.html
[27] http://www.wired.co.uk/article/samsung-knox-security-vulnerabilities
[28] https://www.apple.com/business/docs/iOS_Security_Guide.pdf

delivered a presentation detailing the motivation behind and implementation of several iOS security architecture elements. [29]

These security architecture improvements across all the mainstream mobile and PC operating systems (Google's Android and Apple's iOS as well as Microsoft's Windows and other operating systems) are to be encouraged and applauded because they increase resilience to attack and raise the level of difficulty and the cost for attackers to discover vulnerabilities and develop exploits. Nevertheless, sufficiently motivated parties will continue to find exploitable vulnerabilities in mobile operating systems and other lower-level device components.

The term "zero-day vulnerability" is used to describe vulnerabilities that are not yet known to the vendor and hence have not yet been patched. In September 2015, the security company Zerodium offered a $1 million prize for exploitable vulnerabilities against Apple iOS that met certain criteria; one team won the prize.[30] To encourage disclosure and thank security researchers for their work discovering vulnerabilities, Apple and Google now also offer significant monetary rewards (commonly known as bug bounties) to security researchers who report discovered vulnerabilities. The large monetary value associated with these zero-day vulnerabilities potentially means that they will not be "wasted" on low-value targets, but could still be used by advanced attackers against high-value targets where the investment is justified.

The advanced Apple iOS malware called Pegasus, discovered by Citizen Lab and Lookout in August 2016, serves as a recent example. Citizen Lab's report[31] describes how Ahmed Mansoor, "an internationally recognized human rights defender, based in the United Arab Emirates (UAE)," had his iPhone targeted by Short Message Service (SMS) text messages containing links that led to zero-day exploits that could silently jailbreak his device and install spyware. Citizen Lab and Lookout reported the vulnerabilities to Apple on August 15 and Apple pushed out a new version of iOS (9.3.5) on August 25.

Some users choose to "jailbreak" or "root" their devices, deliberately exploiting vulnerabilities on their mobile device to enable desired capabilities that would otherwise not be available. This process results in the device being placed in a weakened security state that could be exploited by attackers. Figure 5 graphically depicts the findings reported in mobile threat defense vendor Skycure's first quarter 2016 Mobile Threat Intelligence Report: 0.02 percent of enterprise-managed iOS devices and 0.71 percent of enterprise-managed Android devices were jailbroken or rooted, while 0.56 percent of self-managed iOS devices and 3.85

Figure 5. Jailbroken or Rooted Devices

[29] https://www.blackhat.com/docs/us-16/materials/us-16-Krstic.pdf; https://www.youtube.com/watch?v=BLGFriOKz6U
[30] https://www.zerodium.com/ios9.html
[31] https://citizenlab.org/2016/08/million-dollar-dissident-iphone-zero-day-nso-group-uae/

percent of self-managed Android devices were jailbroken or rooted.[32]

Instances have occurred where vulnerabilities are discovered in device, vendor or carrier-specific additions to an operating system. For example, in November 2014, a serious vulnerability was discovered in the SwiftKey third-party keyboard application bundled with many Samsung mobile devices.[33] The vulnerability could be exploited by attackers to obtain remote access to those mobile devices.

Mobile devices typically have strong security dependencies on cloud services provided by the operating system vendor. Exploitation of the cloud services or, more likely, individual account credentials on the cloud services, can be leveraged to exploit mobile devices. For example, Google and Apple provide the Android Device Manager and Find My iPhone (which works on iPads as well) capabilities, respectively. These capabilities allow a device owner to remotely track and, if desired, wipe the data on his or her device and are incredibly valuable in the case of a lost or stolen device. If the device owner's account credentials are compromised, however, the same capability could be abused by an attacker to track the physical location of the device over time or to wipe valuable data from the owner's devices. A prominent example of abuse of this capability was provided by Mat Honan of *Wired*, whose Amazon, Apple, Google, and Twitter accounts were compromised and his data wiped from his Apple devices.[34]

Google also provides a remote capability to install applications onto Android devices by accessing the Google Play Store website from a PC. Security researchers have demonstrated the ability to abuse this capability to deliver malicious applications to Android devices[35] and Symantec described the abuse of this capability by Windows malware in its 2016 Internet Security Threat Report.[36] Use of this attack technique requires an attacker to successfully submit a malicious application to the Google Play Store.

Partly to help mobile device owners recover from a lost or stolen device, devices are often configured to backup device data either to cloud services or to an attached PC. Attackers can potentially gain access to this data as prominently demonstrated by the theft of pictures from the Apple iCloud accounts of celebrities in 2014.[37]

IV.2.1.2 Defenses

The most important defense against mobile device security threats is to ensure devices are patched against publicly known security vulnerabilities and are running the most recent operating system version. Installation of patches ensures that devices cannot be trivially targeted with well-known public exploits, but rather an attacker must invest time, resources, and risk of detection into developing more sophisticated attack methods. Running the most recent operating system ensures devices are benefiting from general security architecture improvements that provide resilience against vulnerabilities that may not yet be publicly known.

---

[32] https://www.skycure.com/wp-content/uploads/2016/06/Skycure-Q1-2016-MobileThreatIntelligenceReport.pdf
[33] https://www.nowsecure.com/keyboard-vulnerability/
[34] http://www.wired.com/2012/08/apple-amazon-mat-honan-hacking/
[35] https://jon.oberheide.org/blog/2011/03/07/how-i-almost-won-pwn2own-via-xss/;
http://www.vvdveen.com/publications/BAndroid.pdf
[36] https://www.symantec.com/content/dam/symantec/docs/reports/istr-21-2016-en.pdf
[37] https://www.wired.com/2014/09/eppb-icloud/

Enterprises should check the operating system version (and Android security patch level in the case of Android devices) of their mobile devices and consider blocking access to sensitive enterprise networks or resources from devices that are out of date.

When making procurement decisions, enterprises should seek a clear commitment from device vendors or mobile carriers that security updates will be provided in a timely manner and devices will continue to be supported with security updates for a set period. When a device model is no longer supported with updates, enterprises should decommission those devices, including sanitization of data stored on the device in accordance with applicable Government policies. Listing on the NIAP Product Compliant List (PCL) is a good indication that a mobile device is supported by the vendor since NIAP policy requires that vulnerabilities be patched for a product to remain listed.

Enterprises should advise users not to deliberately root or jailbreak mobile devices. On Android devices, Google's SafetyNet attestation capability should be used to block access to enterprise resources from devices that are known to be compromised. Samsung KNOX also provides an attestation capability that can be used on Samsung's Android devices. On both Android and iOS devices, numerous enterprise security products provide capabilities to identify artifacts associated with rooted or jailbroken mobile devices. While these checks are not foolproof, they can at least detect the most common techniques.

To defend against threats to cloud services provided by the mobile device vendor or operating system vendor, enterprises should advise users to enable strong authentication methods when available, such as multifactor authentication. On enterprise-owned devices, enterprises also could enforce use of enterprise-managed (rather than user-managed) accounts on cloud services or disable use of unneeded cloud services in favor of services provided by an EMM solution, when feasible.

IV.2.2 Lower-Level Device Components

IV.2.2.1 Threats

The mobile operating system depends on lower-level device components for its secure operation. When the mobile device powers on a component called the bootloader handles loading the operating system code. If the bootloader contains vulnerabilities or is insecurely configured (e.g., is running in an unlocked mode intended only for development use), an attacker could tamper with the operating system code and load an alternate version with malicious behavior.

Without a secure platform, you cannot have privacy—it would be possible to have a secure device that does not address privacy, but not the other way around.

Qualcomm

Mobile devices generally use an isolated execution environment such as a Trusted Execution Environment (TEE) (on Android and some other devices) and Apple's Secure Enclave (on Apple iOS devices) that runs independently from the main operating system (e.g., Android or iOS). These environments provide security-critical capabilities such as storing cryptographic keys, including the keys used to encrypt sensitive data stored on the mobile device. Moving security-critical capabilities to an isolated execution environment provides resilience against attacks that successfully exploit the main operating system. However, even these isolated environments are not necessarily immune from exploitation. Researchers have discovered vulnerabilities in TEE code running on Android devices.[38] In one case, a researcher demonstrated how these vulnerabilities can be exploited to subvert the protections for the Android disk encryption keys.[39]

However, it should be noted that unlike a PC, mobile devices contain several critical elements that do not boot from the core bootloader, but instead from their own internal firmware. Figure 6 depicts these interdependent processors. In addition to the main processor that runs the device's primary operating system, mobile devices include baseband processors that manage network connections, and the SIM. If these elements—which include the cellular and Wi-Fi baseband, the NFC subsystem and others—are trusted by a device they also can serve as sources of attack vectors.[40] Because the software of these components is embedded in the chips themselves, such vulnerabilities can be difficult to remediate.

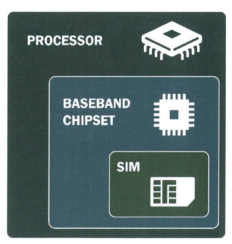

Figure 6. Smartphone Processors

To aid in troubleshooting and customer support, many Mobile Network Operators (MNOs) add software below the mobile operating system (i.e., between the operating system and the firmware) to gain visibility into a device's interaction with their infrastructure. This software is typically outside the purview of the mobile operating system provider, making it difficult to detect. It can also serve as a threat vector that can be updated over the air to add new capabilities.

CarrierIQ[41] is an example of this type of software. Recently, Kryptowire discovered an example of this supply chain issue in an Original Equipment Manufacturer (OEM) product that sent PII, call logs, SMS messages, and contact information to a foreign country without permission, user consent, or user knowledge.[42] This threat type fundamentally compromises the mobile device, which can defeat end-to-end encryption.

IV.2.2.2 Defenses

As with operating system threats, the most important defense against lower-level device component threats is to ensure devices are patched against publicly known security vulnerabilities. Security updates may include patches for both the operating system and lower-level device components. The same defenses listed in Section IV.2.1.2 are applicable here.

Table 2 summarizes available defenses against attacks to mobile device components and their ability to protect (prevent), detect, or respond to those threats.

---

[38] https://usmile.at/symposium/program/2015/thomas-holmes
[39] https://bits-please.blogspot.in/2016/06/extracting-qualcomms-keymaster-keys.html:
[40] Ralf Philipp Weinmann. "WOOT 2012: Baseband Attacks: Remote Exploitation of Memory Corruptions in Cellular Protocol Stacks" (PDF). USENIX WOOT. Retrieved 2015-04-05; http://www.informationweek.com/wireless/nfc-phone-hacking-and-other-mobile-attacks/d/d-id/1105508
[41] https://techcrunch.com/2011/12/01/carrier-iq-how-to-find-it-and-how-to-deal-with-it/
[42] http://arstechnica.com/security/2016/11/chinese-company-installed-secret-backdoor-on-hundreds-of-thousands-of-phones/

Table 2. Available Defenses to Mitigate Attacks Against Device Components

Defense	Description	Protect	Detect	Respond
Install security patches	Ensure that mobile devices are kept up to date with the latest security patches to prevent exploitation of publicly known vulnerabilities. Block access to enterprise resources from devices that are out of date.	*		
Decommission unsupported devices	Replace mobile devices that are no longer supported with new security updates by the vendor or carrier.	*		
Enable device integrity checking capabilities	When available, make use of device integrity checking capabilities such as remote attestation features that can be used to detect and respond to indications of device compromise.		*	*
Acquire only devices that meet security criteria	Seek commitments from the device vendor or mobile carrier at procurement to provide security updates in a timely manner and continue security update support for a set period. Only purchase devices with secure boot capabilities and other critical security features, e.g., as defined in NIAP's Mobile Device Fundamentals Protection Profile.	*		

IV.2.3 Summary of Gaps in Mobile Device Technology Stack Defenses

Despite industry's ongoing efforts to address threats against the mobile operating system and other lower-level mobile device components by continually improving device security architectures and security update processes, gaps remain, including:

- The inability of enterprises to gain visibility into indicators of adversary activity such as indications of exploitation of previously unknown (zero-day) vulnerabilities.
- Variations in security update speed and availability depending on the device vendor or network carrier.
- The inattention to software assurance best practices during the development of some mobile device components.
- The failure to use strong authentication mechanisms—even when available—for cloud services on which the device depends for secure functionality.
- Much effort has gone into increasing the resilience of mobile device components against exploitation, but continued effort is required in this area and should focus not only on the mobile operating system but also on lower-level components such as TEEs and baseband processors and the software/firmware used to operate them.
- Software or firmware installed by the MNO or OEM is typically outside the purview of the mobile operating system provider, making it difficult to detect.

IV.3 Mobile Applications

An application program (application or app for short) is a computer program designed to perform a group of coordinated functions, tasks, or activities for the benefit of the user. Mobile apps allow the user to access the myriad sensors built into their device, read or write information or files stored on their device, and communicate through a variety of channels with other users, other devices, Internet sites, proprietary or Government services, applications, and data stores.

The sheer number of apps available from the major app stores has exploded in the past several years. Apple announced in June 2016 that there are two million apps available on its app store and that apps have been downloaded over 130 billion times since the app store launched in 2008.[43] The Google Play store has a comparable number of apps, with several sources indicating that the store has surpassed Apple in the number of apps available. Other app stores commonly accessed in the U.S.—Windows Store, Amazon Appstore and Blackberry World—account for approximately 1.5 million additional applications.[44]

Most mobile applications are provisioned through public stores owned and operated by the major operating system vendors or provisioned directly to the phone prior to sale by the OEM or cellular carrier. Enterprises also distribute apps via private app stores; these apps are not meant for public distribution but for use within the organization. Third-party stores also exist. These are legitimate and non-legitimate sources of applications, but the reliability and security of apps from these sources may vary widely and the vetting process may be opaque or less robust than is the case for the public stores of OS vendors.

Almost five million apps are available in the major mobile app stores.

Kryptowire LLC

Although app provenance may exacerbate an issue (i.e., getting an app from a third-party app store that specializes in apps for jailbroken or rooted devices significantly increases risk), ultimately apps present risk because of vulnerabilities in the app that are subject to exploitation or because they are intentionally malicious.

Figure 7 provides an overview of the role that applications play in the exploitation of mobile devices. In addition to the threats depicted, the impact of vulnerable apps and impacts to privacy (distributing information about the user or compiling user profiles for targeted marketing) are also considered in the discussion that follows.

---

[43] Apple WorldWide Developer Conference, June 13-17, 2016.
[44] Apps that are offered across multiple platforms may be counted more than once in this assessment.

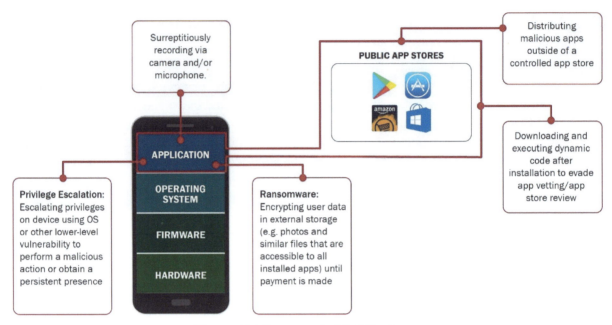

Figure 7. Threats via Mobile Apps

IV.3.1 Vulnerabilities in Mobile Applications

IV.3.1.1 Threats against Vulnerable Applications

Vulnerabilities in applications are usually the result of mistakes or failure to follow secure coding practices. Vulnerabilities present risk when they are exploited—either intentionally or unintentionally—and result in some compromise to a user's data. With proper and thorough code review, these vulnerabilities may be caught during production and prior to release. However, some vulnerabilities are not recognized or discovered until after the application has reached the marketplace. Even when discovered, applications containing these vulnerabilities remain a risk to the user if the application is not updated or removed. Risks introduced by coding errors are mitigated to some extent by the architecture of mobile devices, whereby applications are isolated and therefore are unable by default to interact with other applications or the mobile operating system. However, there are several examples of vulnerabilities in software that expose the user to excessive risk, which include the following.

Insecure Network Communication. If network traffic between an application and a remote server is not securely encrypted an attacker positioned on the network can eavesdrop on the connection, including obtaining sensitive data such as login credentials. An attacker also may be able to perform a man-in-the-middle attack, gaining not only the ability to eavesdrop on the connection but also the opportunity to alter data as it traverses the path, resulting in delivery of compromised information. In some cases, applications use encrypted protocols, but improperly authenticate the identity of the remote server when connecting. This failure also creates the opportunity for man-in-the-middle attacks.

Files Stored with Insecure File Permissions or in an Unprotected Location. Applications with this vulnerability can lead to exposure of sensitive information, often without the user's knowledge. For example, early versions of Skype for Android stored personal data (contacts, profile, message logs) in an unencrypted format and improperly assigned insecure file permissions that allowed anyone or any app to read them. While this vulnerability has since been mitigated (by Skype and via improved protections given to internal storage directories in Android), it is representative of the harm that can occur with minor vulnerabilities in application code.

Sensitive Information Written to System Log. Applications for Android and iOS have been found that write sensitive information into plaintext log files that may be read by attackers. The instances that prompted inclusion in the Common Vulnerabilities and Exposures (CVE) database (CVE-2012-2630 and CVE-2014-0647) revealed Twitter credentials and Starbucks usernames, passwords, and e-mail account information. This threat has largely been mitigated in recent versions of Android and iOS that have stricter access controls to the system log.

Web Browser Vulnerabilities. Vulnerabilities in mobile device web browser applications can be exploited by attackers as an entry point to gain access to a mobile device. For example, the Pegasus malware targeting iOS devices (discussed in Section IV.2.1) exploited vulnerabilities in the Safari web browser after the user was sent a link to a web page containing malicious code. The Dogspectus malware targeting Android devices exploited vulnerabilities in the built-in web browser on Android 4.x to silently and automatically install a ransomware application onto a device.[45] Newer versions of Android and iOS include security architecture improvements designed to make it more difficult for an attacker to exploit web browser vulnerabilities. Backing up data files to an external location and performing a factory reset of the phone can mitigate the attack, but at an expense of time and effort. Updating to a more robust browser is also recommended.

Vulnerabilities in Third-Party Libraries. Third-party software are reusable components that may be distributed freely or offered for a fee to other software vendors. Software development by component or modules is often considered more efficient, and third-party libraries are routinely used across the industry. However, when a library is flawed it can introduce vulnerabilities in any app that includes or makes use of that library. Depending on the pervasiveness of the library, its use can potentially affect thousands of apps and millions of users.

For example, in 2015 an open-source (third-party) library that was used by iOS for communicating with web services had a flaw that disabled the validation of digital certificates when attempting to establish a secure communication channel, allowing a classic man-in-the-middle attack. The vulnerability only affected a specific release of the third-party code and was patched quickly, but some estimates indicate that 1,000 applications were still vulnerable six months after discovery because of failures in the patching process.[46]

Advertisement libraries are a common example of third-party software included in mobile applications. Mobile applications often are distributed for free, with advertisements used as a source of revenue for the developer. Vulnerabilities have previously been found in advertisement libraries, affecting any application using the library. For example, a major vulnerability

---

[45] See: https://www.bluecoat.com/security-blog/2016-04-25/android-exploit-delivers-dogspectus-ransomware
[46] Sourcedna blog.

discovered in the Vungle advertisement library in 2015 could be exploited by an attacker to execute malicious code and remotely gain access to Android mobile devices.[47]

Cryptographic Vulnerabilities. Cryptographic vulnerabilities can occur via failure to use cryptographic protections for sensitive data, by the improper implementation of a secure cryptographic algorithm, or the use of a proprietary cryptographic technique that can be more easily cracked than those validated and recommended for use by NIST. The net result to users, however, is likely to be the same, sensitive information that is presumed secure is potentially exposed to unauthorized users.

IV.3.1.2 Defenses Against Vulnerabilities in Apps

It is important to consider app provenance when discussing the defenses available against apps with inherent vulnerabilities. The two broad classes of applications available to the Federal Government are those commissioned or built specifically for internal or external use (i.e., Government mission or public access to Government data) or commercially available apps that are leveraged for Government use. Mitigations can be broadly described as belonging to one of three types: best practices in development, test cases prior to distribution, and maintenance following implementation.

Government-built or commissioned applications provide an enhanced opportunity and means to control the design and verify the security of applications. Development best practices and standards—where available—should reduce or ideally eliminate known vulnerabilities during the build process. Commercially available applications bring valuable capabilities and can be assessed for potential security vulnerabilities before use.

Some of these practices can be applied during development and others should be enforced during the maintenance phase. These include such things as the following:

- Application developers should be made aware of and should follow security best practices such as those published by Google for Android[48] and Apple for iOS.[49]
- Application developers should make use of free capabilities bundled into the application development environment to assess the security of their applications, e.g., the Android Software Development Kit and the Android Lint capability built into Android Studio.
- Application developers should make use of the Network Security Configuration feature recently introduced into Android[50] and the Application Transport Security feature recently introduced into iOS[51] to protect their apps from inadvertent network communication vulnerabilities.
- Application developers and/or enterprises should consider using commercial mobile application vetting tools that can assess applications for many common vulnerabilities. Many mobile security vendors[52] provide tools in this space; some integrate with threat

---

[47] https://www.nowsecure.com/blog/2015/06/15/a-pattern-for-remote-code-execution-using-arbitrary-file-writes-and-multidex-applications/
[48] https://developer.android.com/training/best-security.html
[49] https://developer.apple.com/library/mac/documentation/Security/Conceptual/SecureCodingGuide/Introduction.html
[50] Android Best Practices for Security and Privacy at developer.android.com
[51] iOS 9 SDK
[52] http://csrc.nist.gov/publications/drafts/nistir-8136/nistir_8136_draft.pdf

intelligence tools to bring more up-to-date information about vulnerabilities or malicious code to the enterprise.

- Respondents to the Mobile Threats and Defenses RFI proposed Software Development Kits (SDKs) that can help ensure appropriate data encryption, strong access control, separation between applications (e.g., restricting copy-paste ability), and provide the ability to perform local or remote data wipes of individual application data. Some of these SDKs provide the ability to add security protections by "wrapping" existing apps.
- Enterprises should deploy and maintain EMM/MDM tools.
- Threat intelligence should be used to understand the potential risks associated with apps installed on devices. It also can be used to develop whitelisted (allowed) and blacklisted (prohibited) apps or app catalogs.
- Ensure devices are running the latest version of iOS or Android because each OS version has brought security architecture improvements and ensure applications receive security patches. Figure 8 shows that many users are slow in updating their devices with the latest Android version,[53] with over 40 percent running KitKat (version 4.4) or earlier versions that are no longer supported.

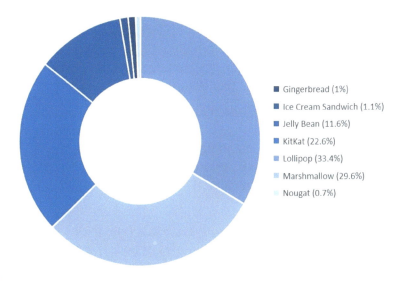

- Gingerbread (1%)
- Ice Cream Sandwich (1.1%)
- Jelly Bean (11.6%)
- KitKat (22.6%)
- Lollipop (33.4%)
- Marshmallow (29.6%)
- Nougat (0.7%)

Figure 8. Android OS Fragmentation

While there are multiple sources for best practices in development and operations, there is neither a standard process nor guidance equivalent to that found for system development that establishes the required security controls based on an assessment of the security categorization of the data. A notable exception is NIAP's Protection Profile for Application Software, which is geared toward applications that implement security functionality on National Security Systems, but is generally applicable to all mobile apps.

In addition to development standards, there are multiple tools available to examine an application prior to deployment based on established techniques for reviewing software. Integrating use of these tools in the development process can increase confidence the app will not exhibit vulnerabilities that may lead to exploitation.

There is a robust community of vendors that supply a variety of tools or services used in the security vetting of mobile applications. These tools generally reflect best practices as determined by the vendor community. Considerable work remains to develop a standard set of criteria—especially one based on use case—and validate the existing tools against those standards.

---

[53] https://developer.android.com/about/dashboards/index.html

Preliminary work has been done to validate tool use against the NIAP Protection Profile for Application Software and its Requirements for Vetting Mobile Apps, but the profile has yet to be adopted as the standard against which apps for Federal Government use are validated in circumstances other than apps that implement security services for National Security Systems. App validation that links to threat intelligence is still a nascent technology.

The technologies and services described in the following paragraphs were initially aimed at web applications and have been adapted to the assessment of mobile apps. While much of the analysis is automated, app security review still requires skilled analysts and manual investigation.

Static Analysis. Static analysis tools examine source code, byte code[54] or binary code line by line to find flaws that make it susceptible to exploit without executing the code. The results of the analysis provide the exact line of code where the flaw resides, providing developers a quick path to remediate the problem. Static analysis tools can produce false-positives because they essentially are comparing code to specific standards; some developers may have produced nonstandard code that is still secure.

Static Source Code Analysis. This method analyzes the source code without running the app. It can detect errors that may not be revealed during dynamic testing because all pathways can be examined, not just those exercised during runtime. This analysis is the only method that can be used effectively on many types of applications (depending on support for specific programming languages and frameworks and availability of source code) and it is especially important for mobile apps.

Static Byte Code Analysis. Static byte code tools operate similar to source code or binary code analysis but at a different level of code.[55] Byte code cannot be executed directly, but is interpreted on a Java virtual machine or compiled for execution in a 'just-in-time' compiler. Byte code analysis (or binary code analysis) may be the only option in instances where source code is not available.

Static Binary Code Analysis. Binary code analysis is used in situations where source code is unavailable. In some respects, this type of analysis views the code more closely aligned to the way it is presented to the end-user. By examining the entire complied code, the reviewer can examine linked libraries, Application Programming Interfaces (APIs), compiler optimizations and third-party components that source code testing cannot identify.

Dynamic Binary Analysis. Dynamic analysis tests and evaluates applications during runtime.[56] Often used as a mechanism for debugging code, it also has uses in evaluating behavior that may be difficult to elucidate from an examination of the source code. Dynamic analysis recently has been used to assess the security of some commercial mobile applications. Many app security teams use Dynamic Application Security Testing (DAST) when testing the security of mobile and web applications because they can implement this technology with little, or sometimes no, involvement from development teams. This "black box" dynamic testing is highly automated and the tests frequently can be run on-demand through a service or tool.

---

[54] Byte code refers to code of an interpreted language like Java or .Net.
[55] Several Java byte-code analysis tools are listed at http://java-source.net/open-source/code-analyzers
[56] See some examples of tools at http://en.wikipedia.org/wiki/Dynamic_code_analysis

In many cases, the Government has less visibility into the software assurance status of commercially available apps. However, the same techniques used for Government app security verification are available to review applications even when the original source code is not available. As with apps developed specifically for the Government, however, failure to find vulnerabilities in an application prior to deployment neither guarantees that vulnerabilities will not be discovered in the future, nor does it provide assurance that subsequent updates to the app will be free of vulnerabilities. Ongoing assurance, based on a common and comprehensive set of security objectives, is necessary throughout the application lifecycle.

A robust development process based on best practices and due diligence in vetting an app for security does not preclude the possibility that vulnerabilities will be discovered after deployment. This leads to the third process for maintaining security in mobile devices: using threat intelligence as well as monitoring and mitigation when vulnerabilities are discovered. Diligence in maintaining currency in device operating systems and applications reduces (but cannot eliminate) the risk that an application will lead to compromise. Understanding the deployed application base and monitoring that those apps continue to be maintained by the developer is a critical part of maintenance. Apps for which vulnerabilities are discovered should be patched as soon as possible or removed from the device if patching is no longer an option.

IV.3.2 Potentially Harmful Applications (Malicious or Privacy-Invasive)

The term Potentially Harmful Applications is adopted from *The Google Android Security Team's Classifications for Potentially Harmful Applications,*[57] which describes "the Android Security Team's taxonomy for classifying apps that pose a potential security risk for users or their data."

IV.3.2.1 Threats from Potentially Harmful Applications

Unlike apps with vulnerabilities that may be exploited by third-parties, harmful applications are intentionally designed to gather or compromise sensitive data. In many cases, this is done without the user's knowledge or acceptance, but in some cases the app requests access to data or services when installed that exceeds the permissions necessary for full functionality without the user's understanding of the consequence.

Colluding mobile apps appear benign but when they run on the same mobile device and share information, they may be malicious. McAfee Labs has discovered app collusion in more than 5,000 installation packages representing 21 mobile apps with a wide range of permissions.

McAfee Labs Threats Report, June 2016

Malicious or privacy-invasive apps often operate by exploiting vulnerabilities in the underlying mobile OS. Threats and potential mitigations related to the OS should therefore be considered in conjunction with the threat from applications.

---

[57] https://static.googleusercontent.com/media/source.android.com/en//security/reports/Google_Android_Security_PHA_classifications.pdf

While new malware is constantly being introduced into the marketplace, the following examples provide a broad overview of the types of malicious actions that are possible and the consequences to Government users and data.

Apps that Gather Privacy-Sensitive Information. These are malicious apps that can collect information such as device persistent identifiers, device location, list of installed applications, contact lists, call logs, calendar data, or text messages without adequate consent of the user. In many cases, the permissions needed to access this information are disclosed upon installation or while the app is running, but users may or may not be aware of the consequences. Often these apps transmit this data to an external source that may be collecting large amounts of data.

Surreptitious Eavesdropping. Some malicious apps are capable of quietly accessing device sensors to eavesdrop or photograph the user or others. As with apps that collect privacy-sensitive information, the permissions necessary to access those components may be disclosed to the user at install, but users may or may not be aware of the consequences.

Exploiting Vulnerabilities. Apps may be designed to take advantage of vulnerabilities in other apps, the operating system, or other device components despite the isolation capabilities of the mobile OS.

Exploiting Access to Sensitive Enterprise Networks or Data. One family of malicious apps that has demonstrated an ability to infiltrate vulnerable networks and databases is called "Not Compatible." This malware allowed attackers to access any network to which the mobile device was connected, including those theoretically protected by VPNs. Another example is the DressCode malware depicted in Figure 9. An infected device connects to the DressCode botnet's command and control server and establishes a secure tunnel with the command and control server. The compromised device then acts as a proxy that relays traffic between the attacker and internal enterprise servers to which the device is connected.[58]

---

[58] http://blog.trendmicro.com/trendlabs-security-intelligence/dresscode-potential-impact-enterprises/

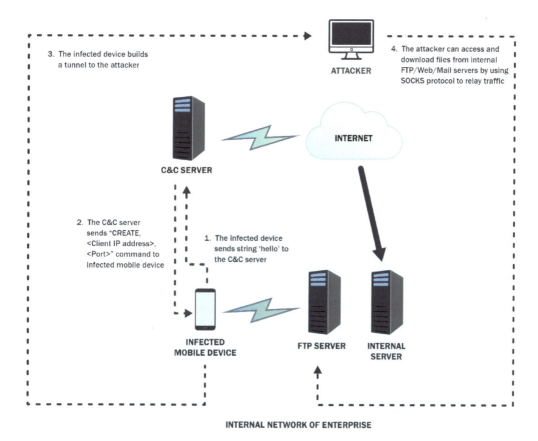

Figure 9. DressCode Malware[59]

Ransomware. Ransomware is a particularly insidious app that in some variants poses as representing a law enforcement agency and demands payment to unlock or decrypt the phone. These apps often are resistant to removal and even when it is possible to mitigate the risk, productivity is lost while the phone is locked. Ransomware attacks are on the rise and are becoming increasingly more sophisticated.

Enabling Other Types of Fraud or Malicious Practices. Apps can attempt to subvert authentication techniques by impersonating the login screens of legitimate apps to obtain account credentials or intercepting and surreptitiously forwarding SMS messages containing authentication codes used by enterprises, financial institutions, or others.

Exploiting Public Mobile Application Stores. Attackers could obtain developer credentials to subvert the developer's identity and reputation and submit new malicious applications or malicious app updates to app stores. Attackers also can seek to evade the screening techniques used by app stores to insert malicious apps without detection. In Lookout's RFI response, it stated that in the second quarter of 2016 alone, it identified 14 separate malicious apps in the Google Play Store that successfully got through Google's review process. Security researchers have demonstrated techniques that can be used to evade the screening processes used by Google and Apple. For example, there have been attacks based on Apple's implementation of enterprise

---

[59] Graphic used with permission of TrendMicro.

35

certificates. These allow enterprises to essentially bypass the Apple App Store to distribute apps directly to the enterprise. While there are many legitimate uses for this technique, it can be abused by third-party stores that register for the program and then claim to be part of another organization.[60]

It should be noted that Google and Apple have made continuous improvements in their security processes, including app vetting, a cornerstone of their business models. (Section IV.2.1)

Attempting to Root/Jailbreak a Mobile Device. Users may attempt to root or jailbreak their device to gain access to application stores that might otherwise be inaccessible. Not only are these third-party application stores more likely to contain malicious applications than the mainstream application stores, the root or jailbreak process often places the device in a degraded security state that could be taken advantage of by attackers. In some instances, users intentionally install applications to jailbreak their device. This allows them to view pirated content and run pirated games. In addition, there are malicious apps that attempt to surreptitiously jailbreak or root devices without a user's knowledge.[61]

Manipulation of Trusted Apps. Malicious applications in the marketplace masquerade as a benign (and often popular) application. Downloaded unwittingly by a user, the app then performs any number of malicious activities without the user's awareness. Some effectively mimic the real app's behavior on the surface, making it difficult for the user to recognize the risks to which they are exposed.

Sharing of Data Between Trusted Apps. Apps may share data with external resources such as Dropbox without the user's awareness.

IV.3.2.2 Defenses Against Potentially Harmful Apps

Defenses can be applied at varying stages of development or deployment as well as throughout the mobile ecosystem to prevent or mitigate risks of potentially harmful mobile applications. Some of the tools described in the following paragraphs are also applicable to the defenses against vulnerable apps, although the Government typically has less visibility in the software design process for apps obtained from commercial marketplaces.

While no single solution provides absolute assurance against the risk posed by potentially harmful apps, the vendor survey identified several industries that claim the ability to fully or partially mitigate the risks posed by these apps. Additionally, many vendors recognize the interconnected nature of the mobile environment and provide solutions that integrate across the ecosystem. Certainly, it is the case that across the breadth of industry solutions known risks can generally be detected and mitigated. As with vulnerabilities, however, there are still zero-day attacks that are difficult to detect and mitigate. Additionally, some malicious apps attempt to evade detection by downloading additional malicious code after the app is installed.

Best Practices. Similar to the situation with threats to PCs, user awareness and training is the first and often the best defense against many threats. Understanding the threat landscape and

---

[60] https://www.blackhat.com/docs/asia-16/materials/asia-16-Bashan-Enterprise-Apps-Bypassing-The-iOS-Gatekeeper-wp.pdf
[61] http://www.digitaltrends.com/mobile/android-trojanized-malware-app-threat-news/

maintaining up-to-date software can be a significant deterrent. The best practices identified for mitigating threats from vulnerable apps are relevant to malicious and privacy-invasive apps. Additionally, users should avoid (and enterprises should prohibit on their devices) sideloading of apps and the use of unauthorized app stores. Android's built-in Verify Apps feature or third-party, mobile threat protection solutions for both Android and iOS can help identify potentially harmful apps installed on devices.

App Vetting. App vetting—the assessment of the security status of an application—plays an important part in the development process and can provide significant additional assurances when considering deployment of third-party applications in a Government environment. As described previously, a variety of techniques are available to conduct app vetting, although some depend on the availability of source code.

Runtime (dynamic) behavioral analysis on emulators and/or hardware devices can monitor what sensors, data, or device information apps are collecting and whether the information is then shared with third parties. This type of monitoring can also determine whether the data transfer happens with or without encryption.

It is possible to analyze mobile app functionality for Android and iOS mobile apps with or without access to source code via the static or dynamic binary analysis techniques described in Section IV.3.1.2.

Isolation Technologies. Both Android and iOS contain built-in enterprise management capabilities that can be used to separate enterprise apps from personal or otherwise less-trusted apps that do not require access to enterprise data. For example, Android for Work is available on most recent Android devices and Samsung KNOX Workspace is available on most Samsung Android mobile devices. Apple iOS has a similar capability using its "managed apps" functionality.

Mobile devices provide isolation protections designed to separate individual applications from one another and control interactions between applications and the underlying device components. These separation technologies provide another degree of protection, e.g., by preventing inadvertent sharing of data between enterprise-use applications and personal-use applications. These technologies may also provide "per-application" VPN capabilities, allowing enterprise-use applications to traverse a VPN tunnel and gain access to enterprise resources, while prohibiting personal-use applications from being able to access an internal enterprise network.

Separation technologies can be used to ensure the privacy of personal uses of a mobile device (e.g., in Bring Your Own Device [BYOD] environments) while still ensuring the enterprise has full control over enterprise applications and data on the device.

Out-of-Band Authentication. Strong user authentication can be employed to ensure malicious applications do not access sensitive resources. "Out-of-Band" authentication grants secure access to online accounts by sending one of the authentication methods, such as a one-time-use code, over a channel that is separate from the standard channel and cannot be observed by a malicious application.

Continuous Authentication. Because the form factor of mobile devices makes them more susceptible to being lost or stolen, it is important to ensure that the user is verified throughout a session. Various prototype solutions have been proposed to continuously gather input from multiple sensors on the mobile device to learn the device owner's behavior patterns and use those patterns to continuously authenticate the user. The premise of these technologies is that malware will fail to subvert the user authentication techniques since it cannot mimic the device owner's behavior patterns. Google has implemented a version of this strategy with Smart Lock, which uses information about trusted Bluetooth devices, trusted places, and on-body detection to reduce the number of required manual screen unlocks. Google had previously determined that many users avoid use of a passcode for screen lock due to the number of times the screen had to be unlocked throughout the day. By reducing that number, Google intends to encourage users to invoke a screen lock mechanism to improve device security.

Mobile Device Management/Enterprise Mobility Management. EMMs can be used to institute policies on mobile devices, many of which can help prevent harmful behaviors by applications. EMMs are typically the mechanism used to activate and manage the isolation technologies described earlier. EMMs can also be used to monitor device state and perform actions such as blocking out of compliance devices from accessing enterprise resources until known issues are resolved. A full description of MDM and EMM technologies is provided in Section IV.6.

NIST provides guidance on MDMs in its Special Publication 800-124 Revision 1: Guidelines for Managing the Security of Mobile Devices in the Enterprise. NIST also provides a practical reference architecture for deploying MDMs in an enterprise via NIST SP 1800-4, which also contains an example policy set for MDM/EMM policies. A variety of settings can be implemented, some of which may be overly restrictive depending on the use case in question. Examples of policies that can be instituted using EMMs include:

- Restrict allowed apps through use of whitelists/blacklists.
- Respond to application noncompliance with automated actions, including notifications, enterprise wipe, profile removal (e.g., email), profile installation (e.g., restrictions) and managed application removal.
- Require end-users to upgrade to a compliant OS and send notifications to devices to prompt upgrades and patches.
- Restrict device settings through over-the-air profiles.
- Restrict use of device hardware features such as camera, Secure Digital (SD) card, USB, Bluetooth, tethering and more.
- Disable access to public app stores.
- Disable Facebook and other carrier pre-installed apps.
- Control Wi-Fi, hot spot, and other network security settings.
- Disable content sharing—copy-paste, email, print, open with specific apps.
- Configure email security settings, including disabling copy-paste and SD card access.

Not all of these policies are appropriate for all enterprise environments because each may impact device usability.

EMMs also typically can interface with third-party data sources, including services that provide threat intelligence data about potential security issues with mobile apps.

On-Device, Third-Party Security Applications. Third-party security vendors provide applications that can be used to perform some level of enterprise monitoring of the behavior of other applications installed on the device. These third-party security applications may provide the capability to monitor network usage of other applications or attempts to access privacy-sensitive resources. These applications may be able to interface with threat intelligence sources provided by the vendor to detect the presence of known harmful applications. Because of the security architecture of mobile operating systems, there are limitations in the ability of these types of applications to monitor activity.

Network Monitoring. As an illustration that detection and mitigation against malicious behavior occurs through the mobile ecosystem, network monitoring can be used to indicate the presence of an active threat due to unauthorized data, pictures, audio, video, etc. being transmitted to unauthorized/unknown servers on the Internet. If traffic is cleartext, proof of what was transmitted will be available. If the traffic is encrypted, the destination and other meta-data is still collected. Network behavioral analysis can also identify suspicious traffic patterns to new and/or blacklisted destination IP addresses, at which point the device can be quarantined or wiped.

App Store Mitigations. Apple and Google have made commitments to security and privacy and have implemented tools and services to identify and, when appropriate, remove vulnerable or malicious apps from their respective app stores and/or devices. With their combined market share, this commitment helps mitigate threats for the majority of apps downloaded in the U.S.

Google has implemented the Verify Apps feature, which identifies potentially harmful apps and warns the user prior to installation. It also can prompt the user to remove potentially harmful apps if found on the device and may remove those apps without user intervention if Google determines the apps have no benefit to the user. Should a harmful app be installed and result in compromise of the device security model, Verify Apps can also disable the app.

Apple publishes guidance on the types of apps that are permissible or subject to rejection for its App Store. It notes that apps and developers that abuse security guidance will be removed from its App Store and Developer Program. Apple's security review is proprietary, but it has been responsive to the discovery of potentially harmful apps, removing more than 300 infected apps after it was determined that a compromised third-party library that allowed exfiltration of user data had been used in their creation.

Table 3 summarizes available defenses against application-based attacks and indicates their ability to protect (prevent), detect, or respond to those threats.

Table 3. Available Defenses to Mitigate Application-Based Threats

Defense	Description	Protect	Detect	Respond
Follow application development security best practices	Train developers to follow application security best practices, for example those published by Google for Android and Apple for iOS.	*		
Follow user security best practices	Users should ensure both the OS and apps are updated as soon as possible. Installing updates is an easy way for users to be involved in protecting their security. Users should avoid—and enterprises should prohibit on their devices—sideloading of apps and the use of unauthorized app stores.	*		

Defense	Description	Protect	Detect	Respond
Use application vetting tools or application threat intelligence services	App developers and enterprises can use app-vetting tools that automate assessments of mobile apps for common vulnerabilities and potentially harmful behaviors. Additionally, enterprises can use application threat intelligence services that can identify and respond to known harmful applications installed on mobile devices.	*	*	*
Device built-in isolation technologies	Enterprises can use built-in device technologies such as Android for Work, Apple iOS managed apps, or Samsung Knox Workspace to provide a level of separation between enterprise apps and potentially harmful personal apps installed on managed mobile devices.	*		
Out-of-Band authentication	Strong user authentication can be employed to ensure malicious applications do not access sensitive resources.	*		
Continuous authentication	Largely in the prototype stage, continuous authentication thwarts malicious users or apps as they attempt to falsely authenticate as the user.	*		
Mobile Device Management/Enterprise Mobility Management	MDMs and EMMs can be used to institute policies on mobile devices, many of which can help prevent harmful app behaviors. When combined with threat intelligence, they can respond to threats and take a variety of corrective/mitigating actions. Implementation of whitelisting/blacklisting will also limit exposure to disallowed apps.	*	*	*
On-device, third-party security solutions	Third-party security applications may provide the capability to monitor network usage of other apps or attempts to access privacy-sensitive resources. These products may be able to interface with threat intelligence sources to detect the presence of known harmful apps.	*	*	*
Network monitoring	Network monitoring potentially can detect the transmission of sensitive information to unauthorized or unknown destinations. When used in concert with other technologies, this can lead to new threat intelligence and mitigation actions.		*	

Defense	Description	Protect	Detect	Respond
App store mitigations	Apple and Google have made commitments to security and privacy and have implemented tools and services to identify and—where appropriate—remove vulnerable or malicious apps from their app stores and/or devices.	*	*	*

IV.3.3 Summary of Gaps in Mobile Application Defenses

Despite the efforts of the Government and the commercial sector to address the increasing threat landscape with app vetting and threat intelligence tools and services, gaps remain, including:

> *The caller ID display is unauthenticated and can be made to display any data, including fraudulent information.*
>
> FCC Consumer Guide, Spoofing and Caller ID

- Fragmented toolsets (e.g., modularization of solution sets) hindering the security and implementation of security throughout the lifecycle of mobile applications.
- Poorly defined set of best practices and security Systems Development Life Cycle for developers—especially for Government use.
- Lack of focus on mobile application vulnerabilities within the CVE process.
- Lack of robust information sharing of threat intelligence and integration with security tools and techniques.
- Timely notification to organizations and developers of apps affected by a vulnerability.
- Limited visibility and adoption of application-vetting criteria.[62]
- Lack of formalized standards relating security controls to data security categorization.
- Limited knowledge of the comparison between various app vetting tools.
- Lack of enterprise view into the user community and mobile landscape baseline.

IV.4 Mobile Networks

Vulnerabilities in this element of the mobile ecosystem are the most difficult to remediate because they are an intrinsic part of the design and operation of live cellular networks. Attempts to fix or update deployed systems can lead to outages that can affect the entire country. For this reason, some weaknesses, if deemed minor, may best be left in place or at least left alone until other updates must occur. The vulnerabilities described in the following sections are difficult to remediate, potentially taking months or even years to fully correct.

It is important to note that each generation and family of mobile networks is a unique implementation and is not forward or backward compatible. For a mobile phone or "user equipment" to work on any network it must fully support that network type and the frequency or band over which it operates. For this reason, modern smartphones may contain more than a half-

---

[62] https://www.niap-ccevs.org/pp/pp_app_v1.2_table-reqs.htm

dozen different radios,[63] each designed to operate on a different network type and each with its own firmware. Each radio can be vulnerable to different attacks, including attacks that enable eavesdropping, denial of service of the cellular mobile device and of the network itself, and attacks that can take over total operation of the device.[64] Attacks via this vector appear to be common,[65] although detection is rare.

The most recent generation, LTE, is one of the most robust communication systems deployed at scale in history. It evolved from GSM through UMTS to the current standard. Because of the limited capabilities of early mobile phones, the original design principle was "minimum strength to provide adequate security."[66] Over time this design principle and the resulting security implementations have not withstood advances in attack techniques[67] and the increasing speed of computers used for decryption.[68]

Although the security of LTE is significantly more advanced than GSM, GSM is still widely deployed around the world and will continue operation in the U.S. until at least 2020.[69] This situation means weaknesses inherent in the design of GSM are and will continue to be a risk for the foreseeable future. Even after U.S. carriers shut down GSM service, any phones still in use that support the standard will be vulnerable to attacks from rogue base stations. Given the lifespan of mobile phones[70] —especially those offering global service—this risk will continue for at least a decade and U.S. citizens, especially Government employees assigned to overseas duty stations, will remain vulnerable long after that.

Furthermore, some of the GSM architectural weaknesses have been carried into UMTS (typically referred to as 3G or 4G in the U.S.) and LTE.[71] Some known security issues are even greater in LTE.[72] Additionally, when the GSM encryption and authentication protocols were first defined, the use of the strongest of these was banned for export to many countries.[73] This restriction means some networks in other countries that are likely used by overseas Federal employees still operate with inadequate protection.

Another challenge with LTE is the process of moving from design to manufacturing to implementation. At each step, differences and levels of abstraction occur between the development of the protocol's specifications into the design and construction of the devices and how subsequent rounds of corporations elect to deploy them to implement their customer-facing

---

[63] http://www.chipworks.com/about-chipworks/overview/blog/apple-iphone-7-teardown
[64] https://www.usenix.org/system/files/conference/woot12/woot12-final24.pdf
[65] http://www.welivesecurity.com/2014/08/28/android-security-2/
[66] Dr. Michael Walker, first chairman of the ETSI technical committee Security, p. xvii LTE Security by Dan Forsberg, Günther Horn, Wolf-Dietrich Moeller, Valtteri Niemi
[67] Solutions to the GSM Security Weaknesses, Proceedings of the 2nd IEEE International Conference on Next Generation Mobile Applications, Services, and Technologies (NGMAST2008), pp.576–581, Cardiff, UK, September 2008, arXiv:1002.3175
[68] "A5/1 Cracking Project". Archived from the original on 25 December 2009. Retrieved 30 December 2009.
[69] https://www.rvmobileinternet.com/the-end-is-coming-att-reminds-customers-about-upcoming-2g-network-shutdown/
[70] https://www.cta.tech/News/Blog/Articles/2014/September/The-Life-Expectancy-of-Electronics.aspx
[71] Is the Session Mix-up Attack on the UMTS/LTE AKA Protocol Practical? TTM4905 Report Master Thesis. Norwegian University of Science and Technology Autumn 2012.
[72] p.4, LTE radio transport security: Vulnerabilities, threats and controls, Nokia Networks white paper, http://resources.alcatel-lucent.com/asset/200321
[73] http://www.forbes.com/sites/andygreenberg/2011/08/12/codebreaker-karsten-nohl-why-your-phone-is-insecure-by-design/#7000f9562b56

network. Errors can occur at each abstraction point, commonly leading to the final solution failing to implement critical security requirements spelled out in preceding levels.[74]

To fully realize the security risks in mobile networks, one must first understand the basic design and key components that comprise a mobile network. All mobile networks in use today, regardless of their generation, contain the same fundamental network architecture. Figure 10 depicts the three main components of all cellular networks: the Radio Access Network (RAN), the network core, and services that may or may not be provided by the mobile network operator.

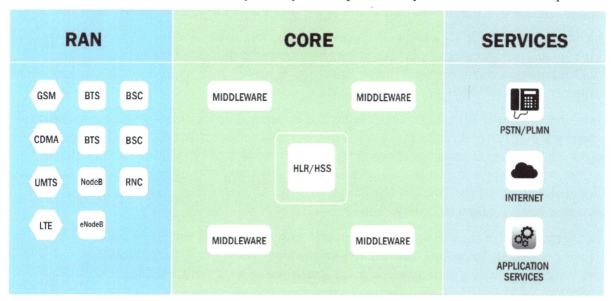

Figure 10. Mobile Network Architecture

Mobile networks generally operate across three planes: voice, data, and control. In LTE, voice and data both run as IP, while in past networks they were separate. The control plane is always out of band; the cellular mobile device has no access to it and it runs on different channels. Within the core network, control plane traffic typically runs on dedicated networks reserved exclusively for its use. Signaling System 7 (SS7) is the historic control plane for mobile networks; although in Voice over IP (VoIP) networks, including LTE, it has been supplanted by the Diameter Protocol, although most networks use both and it is common for SS7 messages to be "translated" into their Diameter equivalent.

The RAN is the part of the mobile network that connects mobile subscribers to their service provider network using Radio Frequency (RF) signaling over an "air interface," i.e., wirelessly. The RAN typically includes tower antennas, RF transceivers and RF controllers. To protect the privacy of callers, this part of the service is typically encrypted, although the level of encryption varies from network type to network type and by decisions the carrier makes in implementing this capability. Different levels of protection exist and vary widely by country.

---

[74] On LTE Security: Closing the Gap Between Standards and Implementation. https://web.wpi.edu/Pubs/ETD/Available/etd-050815-095939/unrestricted/DeMarinis_On_LTE_Security.pdf

The 3GPP standards do not mandate that encryption be enabled by default on the air interface or backhaul network connections. Encryption is an operator option enabled on a case-by-case basis.

The air interface is the only part of the communication stream that is typically encrypted by the carrier. As soon as the signal is converted from RF to wireline at the tower the signal is no longer encrypted by the network. This change means any attacker who gains access at this point can easily eavesdrop on all communications traffic that is not protected by an additional layer of encryption,[75] including the mobile device itself. Such protection is called end-to-end encryption and provides some defense against eavesdropping on all communications platforms.

The data between the RAN and the operator's core network is handled by the backhaul network. This network is responsible for connecting a single tower to the rest of the network system. Backhaul may consist of physical connections (e.g., Ethernet, fiber, coax, etc.), RF transmissions using microwave technology, or a combination.

The Core Network (CN) holds network logic and is responsible for creating and maintaining the connection between cellular mobile devices and external service networks (e.g., Internet, wireline phones, other carriers and private enterprises) as well as physically tracking all user equipment at all times to enable routing of calls and data streams as users and their devices move throughout the landscape. The CN transfers user data and control data, authenticates user devices, manages billing records, and enforces quality of service.

The external service networks contain additional end-user services and may include connections to Public Switched Telephone Network (PSTN) or VoIP networks, Internet browsing, interconnection to other providers (roaming), enterprise specific networks, and "over-the-top" service providers (e.g., Google, Facebook, Apple, etc.).

IV.4.1 SIM Card

The Universal Integrated Circuit Card (UICC) is the current generation SIM card used in modern cellular mobile devices and the foundation of cellular security. As with many platforms in communication and computing, SIMs have evolved and been updated since their introduction two and a half decades ago. Older 2G SIM cards (non-UICCs) cannot access newer networks. Although the term "SIM" is still commonly used, technically all SIMs in use today are Universal Subscriber Identity Modules (USIMs).

UICCs are small computers bonded to a plastic card that are removable from cellular mobile devices by design. Service from a MNO is tied to a user's UICC and, in fact, the MNO legally owns the SIM/USIM. This device communicates directly with the carrier's core network to authenticate itself, the user, and the user's services and service level. In some cases, it is necessary to remove the SIM from a phone frozen in a hung state,[76] which may occur from an unknown fault or an intentional denial of service attack.[77]

---

[75] NISTIR 8071: LTE Architecture Overview and Security Analysis
[76] https://www.verizonwireless.com/support/knowledge-base-112724/
[77] Slide 20, https://www.internetsociety.org/sites/default/files/06_5-ndss2016-slides.pdf

The UICC hosts the USIM application. It performs the full range of security-critical operations required of cellular networks such as authentication and other cryptographic functions,[78] while also providing the capability of storing contacts and other data. The UICC houses a processor— Read-Only Memory (ROM), Random-Access Memory (RAM)—that is network aware and is capable of running Java applications used for a variety of functions ranging from roaming negotiation, updates, and even video games. The UICC potentially can be used for identity services and NFC.

IV.4.1.1 Threats

From a security perspective, one of the most important functions of the UICC is cryptographic key and credential storage. UICCs are provisioned with a long-term, pre-shared cryptographic key used to access the network. This key is stored within the tamper resistant UICC and within the core network's Home Subscriber Server (HSS) and is meant to never leave either of those locations.

A subcomponent of the HSS is the authentication center, which is security-critical. Should an attacker gain access to the key, he or she can access or impersonate the account and subscriber services. UICCs therefore must be manufactured, transported, distributed and installed in a secure environment and the key store must always be protected. International incidents have been reported of key theft and subscriber services fraud. Typically, in the United States this activity has been limited to identity theft of individual accounts.

As shown in Figure 11, SIM cards must pass through at least three entities as they move though the supply chain.[79] Mobile network operators legally own them and the software they contain but do not manufacture them. SIMs are made to specifications supplied by the MNO to the smart card manufacturer. They are then shipped to a card issuer, and distributed to retail outlets that physically dispense them to the MNO's customers. In some cases, additional information is shared with trusted service managers who also have access to the SIMs. All current SIMs can receive over-the-air updates. Any of these steps or handoffs may lead to compromise of the SIM.

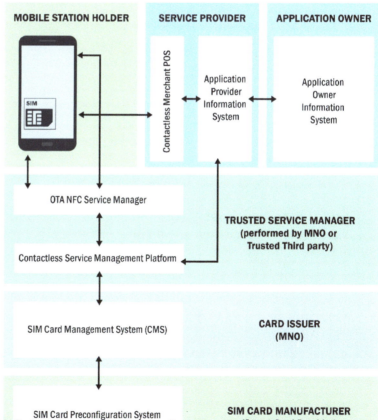

---

[78] 3GPP TS 33.103 V3.4.0 3rd Generation Partnership Project; Technical Specification Group Services and System Aspects; 3G security; Integration guidelines http://www.3gpp.org/ftp/tsg_sa/WG3_Security/_Specs/33103-420.pdf
[79] mobile NFC technical guidelines Version 2.0 November 2007.

Obtaining Cryptographic Keys. Cryptographic keys enable LTE to provide many of the strong security features built into the system. There are many different keys used to protect different layers of LTE communication. All of these keys are derived from a secret pre-shared key referred to as 'K'. This key resides in two places: 1) the USIM running on the UICC; and, 2) within the carrier's HSS authentication center. Depending on **Figure 11. SIM Card Supply Chain** how K is provisioned to the UICC, it may be possible for an attacker to gain access to this secret key. If an attacker gains access to K, he or she has the potential to impersonate a subscriber on the network and the ability to decrypt communication from the subscriber for whom K was provisioned. The processes used to generate these keys—and store them internally—are largely unknown and ungoverned.

SIM Theft. Because UICCs are quickly and easily removed from most phones, it is possible for a UICC to be stolen from one cellular mobile device and placed into another with the goal of stealing service, including voice and data. Another means of stealing service is if an insider with access to the HSS or Policy and Charging Rules Function (PCRF) grants unapproved access to the network. For example, this could be an employee who illicitly activates UICCs and sells them for personal profit. Furthermore, identity theft can also result in a SIM being reissued to a criminal who should not be authorized to use the account.[80]

SIM Cloning. UICCs are difficult to clone without access to the key store. Earlier SIMs could be readily cloned, but these types are rarely used now because of this vulnerability. Although SIMs are based on standards they do vary widely in feature sets and hardening. Some current production SIMs are vulnerable to side-channel attacks and can be cloned, however, this type of attack requires specialized equipment and can take more than an hour per SIM.[81]

IV.4.1.2 Defenses

Users are unlikely to detect that their UICC has been cloned without a review of their billing records, however, even a review may not reveal the issue. The best defense against this threat is anti-fraud systems deployed by the carrier, but these systems do not detect eavesdropping of services, just service theft.

IV.4.2 Radio Access Networks

Denial of Service/Jamming. The wireless connection from the cellular mobile device to the network tower is susceptible to jamming on the up link and the down link. This can be accomplished in a room-sized area using a small battery-powered device or over a much larger area with vehicle mounted systems with dedicated power.

Base stations, or more colloquially "towers," may have physical (e.g., fiber optic) or wireless (e.g., microwave) links to other base stations. These links often are used to perform call handoff operations. "Base station" is a standards-agnostic term referring to a cellular tower communicating with a cellular mobile device, and is used when discussing the interaction between 2G, 3G, and 4G systems. Each set of standards uses a specific term for base station;

---

[80] https://www.ftc.gov/news-events/blogs/techftc/2016/06/your-mobile-phone-account-could-be-hijacked-identity-thief
[81] https://www.blackhat.com/docs/us-15/materials/us-15-Yu-Cloning-3G-4G-SIM-Cards-With-A-PC-And-An-Oscilloscope-Lessons-Learned-In-Physical-Security.pdf

LTE employs the term evolved Node B, which is shortened to eNodeB. Within LTE networks, it may be possible to jam the wireless connections eNodeBs use to communicate with each other. Although theoretical, the same type of smart jamming attacks used against the cellular mobile device could be modified to target communicating eNodeBs, which would prevent the transmission of eNodeB-to-eNodeB RF communication.

The 3GPP SA3 Working Group, the group that defines LTE security standards, says this attack "can be made with special hardware and countermeasures for these are not feasible to implement. However, jamming attacks may be detected and reported."[82] This statement indicates that these types of jamming attacks are outside of the LTE threat model. Proof-of-concept Denial of Service (DoS) attacks have targeted resource request channels on towers using firmware-modified cellular mobile devices. Essentially, this attack impersonates large numbers of phones by forging both the International Mobile Subscriber Identity (IMSI) and International Mobile Equipment Identifier (IMEI) and constantly having the phones make new requests.[83]

Physical Attacks on Base Station Infrastructure. The cell site is the physical location containing all the equipment necessary to run and operate a cellular base station or tower. Although these sites may be protected with physical measures such as a fence and a physical security system, a successful breach of these measures could result in a denial of service attack if the equipment used to run the cellular base station is taken offline or somehow destroyed. Subtler attacks that are much more difficult to detect are also possible if an attacker can gain control of the systems running the cellular base station. It is of note that 3GPP standards allow for backhaul encryption to be disabled if a base station is physically protected, which may just mean the use of fences and typical locks. However, in the United States towers are typically owned by holding companies and most servicing is outsourced, which means that potentially dozens of companies and hundreds of people have access to most towers in a network.[84] Cellular mobile devices regularly switch between types of networks that are used for communication. Unencrypted Wi-Fi networks, regularly deployed and used by the public at locations such as restaurants and airports, are trivial for an attacker to eavesdrop on or manipulate. Encrypted Wi-Fi networks and cellular networks are subject to potential threats as well. Beyond the "first hop" between cellular mobile devices and the nearest Wi-Fi access point or cellular base station, sophisticated attackers may seek to exploit network communications from within core network components.

Long Term Evolution (LTE). The draft NISTIR 8071 report provides an excellent overview of the evolution of cellular network security from the 2G standard to today's widely used LTE standard. LTE has capabilities for mutual authentication and encryption between cellular mobile devices and cellular base stations (eNodeBs). However, cellular mobile devices must maintain backward compatibility with older, less secure cellular network standards to obtain connectivity in cases when LTE service is not available. Attackers can take advantage of this backward compatibility by blocking access to LTE eNodeBs, forcing cellular mobile devices to connect using the less secure standards that are easier to exploit (i.e., a downgrade attack). The following paragraphs describe types of attacks on LTE:

---

[82] 3rd Generation Partnership Project, System Architecture Evolution (SAE): Security Architecture, 3GPP TS 33.401 V12.12, 2014. http://www.3gpp.org/DynaReport/33401.htm

[83] http://mirider.com/Playing_with_the_GSM_RF_Interface-Dieter_Spaar.pdf

[84] http://wirelessestimator.com/top-100-us-tower-companies-list/

Downgrade Attacks.[85] Using a rogue base station broadcasting either close to the cellular mobile device or at a high-power level, an attacker can force a user to downgrade to either GSM or UMTS.[86] As of the time of this writing, there are no significant and publicly known exploitations of the cryptographic algorithms used to protect the confidentiality and integrity of the UMTS air interface. Weaknesses do exist, however, for the 2G GSM cryptographic algorithms used to protect the confidentiality and integrity of the air interface. Examples of broken 2G cryptographic algorithms are A5/1 and A5/2.[87] Depending on the algorithm negotiated while attaching to the rogue base station, the algorithms chosen to protect the air interface may be cryptographically broken, leading to a loss of call and data confidentiality.

Eavesdropping. The cellular mobile device and the eNodeB communicate use an RF connection commonly referred to as the air interface. An eavesdropping attack is possible if the operator does not encrypt user-plane LTE traffic on the air interface; such encryption is not mandated by 3GPP standards. To conduct such an attack, attackers would need to have the proper equipment to capture and store the radio communication between the cellular mobile device and eNodeB. In addition, the attackers would need software to identify the specific LTE frequencies and timeslots a cellular mobile device is using to communicate so they can demodulate the captured traffic into IP packets.

Device and Identity Tracking. It is commonplace today for individuals to constantly keep their cellular mobile devices physically near them, so if the device can be geolocated, the location of the individual can be deduced from that information. Modern smartphones can be located using a wide range of techniques, however, this section will focus solely on network methodologies. For any phone to make or receive a call, the network must know the approximate location of the cellular mobile device. This in turn means any attacker who can gain access to the network, eavesdrop on network traffic, or impersonate the network can obtain this information.[88]

Both the IMSI and IMEI are values that act as unique identifiers on networks. Both identifiers can be combined with other information to identify who owns a cellular device and the device's general physical location. All data needed for geolocation is available via signaling channels and is sent unencrypted over the air interface during the device attach and authentication process.[89] Additionally, inherent to broadcast communications is the potential to use triangulation to identify and geolocate the source of the signal.

The IMSI and IMEI can be determined in several ways including the use of a rogue base station.[90] Rogue base stations are unlicensed base stations that are not operated by an authentic mobile network operator. They broadcast a cellular service masquerading as a legitimate carrier network. The necessary hardware to construct these devices can be obtained inexpensively using commercial off-the-shelf (COTS) hardware. The software required to operate a GSM, UMTS, LTE, or Code Division Multiple Access (CDMA) 2000 base station is open source and freely

---

[85] https://en.wikipedia.org/wiki/Downgrade_attack
[86] https://www.internetsociety.org/sites/default/files/06_5-ndss2016-slides.pdf
[87] Dan Forsberg, G.H., Wolf-Dietrich Moeller, Valtteri Niemi, LTE Security. 2nd ed. 2012: Wiley.
[88] http://arstechnica.com/business/2012/02/location-tracking-of-gsm-cellphones-now-easier-and-cheaper-than-ever/
[89] https://www.internetsociety.org/sites/default/files/06_5-ndss2016-slides.pdf
[90] http://www.ee.columbia.edu/~roger/ShmooCon_talk_final_01162016.pdf

available[91] and can be configured to operate as a rogue base station. Some of these can be quite small, concealable, and operate off battery power.[92]

If a rogue base station is used to intercept traffic in an area such as a user's residence, the operator of the rogue network may be able to identify whether a specific individual is or is not at a specific location or may simply associate the IMSI and IMEI with a specific individual. Alternatively, this information can be used simply to tie a phone to a user; this allows use of other techniques to attack, geolocate, or eavesdrop on the user. Figure 12 depicts a vehicle-mounted IMSI catcher as an example of a cell tower simulator.[93]

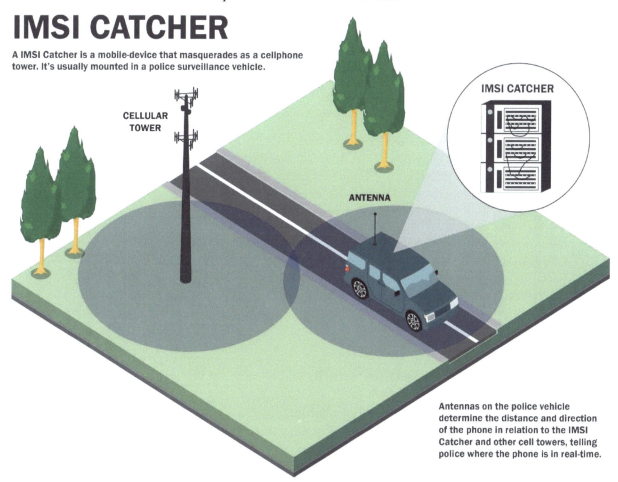

Figure 12. IMSI Catcher Example

Rogue base stations exploit the fact that cellular mobile devices will attach to whichever base station is broadcasting as its preferred carrier network and is transmitting at the highest power level. Therefore, when a rogue base station is physically near to a cellular mobile device while transmitting at a higher power level than the real network base station, the cellular mobile device may attempt to connect to the malicious network. At the time of this writing, most rogue base

---

[91] Range Networks, *OpenBTS Project*, 2015. http://openbts.org
[92] https://secenv.seclab.tuwien.ac.at/secenv/static/inetsec1/11_mobileNetworks.pdf
[93] http://resources.infosecinstitute.com/stingray-technology-government-tracks-cellular-devices/

stations broadcast a 2G GSM cellular network and are widely available.[94] GSM's security protections lack mutual authentication between the cellular mobile device and cellular network and also lack strong cryptographic algorithms with keys of sufficient length.[95] Additionally, there is no requirement mandating encryption of the 2G GSM air interface.

Preventing Emergency Phone Calls. Attackers using a rogue base station could prevent attached cellular mobile devices from accessing emergency services. This occurs when the rogue station fails to forward user traffic to the MNO. If this type of attack occurs during an emergency, it could prevent victims from receiving assistance from public safety services and first responders.

This attack type takes advantage of another vector that comes into play while making emergency phone calls when the preferred network is not available. When making an emergency phone call the cellular mobile device might attach and attempt to send the call through a rogue base station even if the base station is not masquerading as a legitimate network. There is a high risk that the rogue base station will not forward the emergency call appropriately or interfere or block geolocation of the user.

Rogue base stations can also interfere with network-assisted location services by failing to interoperate with the service correctly. GPS units in smartphones need this service to quickly and reliably determine their location.[96] This would mean both the mobile phone and the emergency call center would lack adequate location information to dispatch services.

Rogue base station attacks may or may not be detectable, depending on the level of sophistication of both the cellular mobile device and the rogue unit. Some new cellular mobile devices as well as user installable software on some smartphones attempt to detect rogue base stations, however, these are emerging capabilities.[97] In primitive attacks, since the cellular mobile device believes it has cellular service but is unable to make calls or send/receive data, such an attack will be obvious. More sophisticated attacks can be difficult to distinguish from authorized mobile services.

Network Level Denial of Service (DoS) Attacks. A growing number of DoS and distributed denial of service (DDoS) attacks against the RAN have been discovered and publicly reported. Some of the most significant threats involve attacking the network using botnets.[98] Botnets are collections of compromised devices acting under the control of a central command system.[99] In the case of cellular networks, this typically means compromised Android devices. To date, most Android botnets have been focused on fraud and theft of private data, however, most are modular and can be updated with new attack functions.[100] At least one Android botnet has had persistence and been upgraded for several years.[101]

---

[94] https://www.schneier.com/blog/archives/2015/04/the_further_dem_1.html
[95] https://secenv.seclab.tuwien.ac.at/secenv/static/inetsec1/11_mobileNetworks.pdf
[96] http://www.rohde-schwarz-wireless.com/documents/LTELBSWhitePaper_RohdeSchwarz.pdf
[97] https://www.wired.com/2014/09/cryptophone-firewall-identifies-rogue-cell-towers/
[98] http://web2-clone.research.att.com/export/sites/att_labs/techdocs/TD_101153.pdf
[99] https://en.wikipedia.org/wiki/Botnet
[100] http://www.iosrjournals.org/iosr-jce/papers/AETM'15_CSE/3/24-CSE-155.pdf
[101] http://www.computerworld.com/article/2849689/android-botnet-could-pose-threat-to-corporate-networks.html

Additionally, there are a number of known weaknesses in the various cellular networks that make them vulnerable to DoS and DDoS attacks that are specific to the network type. This includes signaling amplification attacks, HSS saturation attacks, and smart jamming attacks.[102] Other types of attacks that have been described at length elsewhere include ATTACH REJECT messages outlined by NIST and quality of service Class Identifier systems.[103]

IV.4.3 Backhaul Networks

The backhaul network can provide an attacker access to all the control and data traffic sent between cellular mobile devices located in a specific coverage area. The attacker can access a large coverage area by accessing a point within the backhaul network that services multiple cellular towers.

In most mobile networks, towers act as a termination point for encryption protocols used over the wireless RF interface to a cellular device. If physical access to the tower is gained, the data inside the tower can be relatively easy to read or modify and provides the attacker access to both signaling and user communications going to and from the cellular tower. Figure 13 illustrates the distributed geography of a typical cellular network. Cellular networks are spread across the landscape and typically consist of hundreds or thousands of cell towers, each with their own 'blockhouse', which is connected to the core network by backhaul cables that may stretch for hundreds of miles.[104]

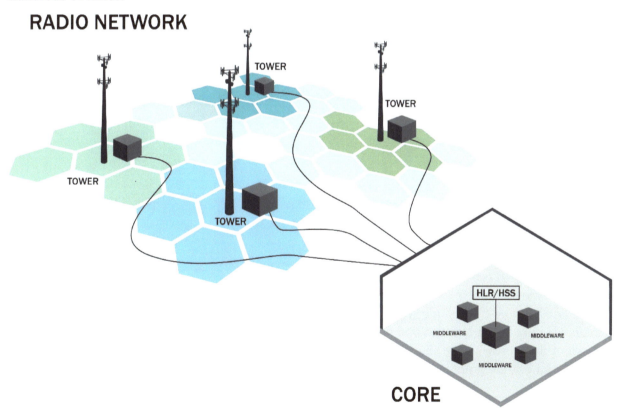

[102] http://web2-clone.research.att.com/export/sites/att_labs/techdocs/TD_101153.pdf
[103] http://riverpublishers.com/journal/journal_articles/RP_Journal_2245-1439_323.pdf
[104] http://www.radio-electronics.com/info/cellulartelecomms/cellular_concepts/cellular-network-basics.php

Figure 13. Distributed Cellular Network

The attacker may be required to physically break into a base station or locate and tap into the backhaul cabling, which may be a difficult task. Some network deployments use microwave technology to establish backhaul connectivity and the attacker may attempt to collect/intercept these microwave signals to access user signaling and data.

In recent years, the mobile industry has increased its support of a new "small cells" approach to expanding coverage area and increasing user capacity. These small cells are generic, mostly Linux-based, home router-like devices developed by third-party vendors. These small cells use common backhaul connections (usually public Internet lines) to connect directly to the core network. Attacking a small cell may provide the attacker a much more convenient way of gaining access to the backhaul (versus breaking into a tower location) and possibly the core network. Over the past few years, several cases were reported where such devices have been hacked or compromised.[105] In 2013, a Verizon Femtocell was reported to be hacked by security researchers to demonstrate their ability to eavesdrop on cellular calls and text messages using the hacked device.[106]

Backhaul Eavesdropping. If an LTE network is not using confidentiality protection on the backhaul interface, the communication being sent to and received from cell sites is vulnerable to eavesdropping.

IV.4.4 Core Networks

For an attacker, compromising the core network would provide virtually unlimited options and attack vectors. Full access is not needed to engage in a wide variety of attacks, especially those seeking only to disrupt services. For example, a DoS attack has been demonstrated against the core authentication system using a botnet to disrupt service for an entire carrier.[107]

AdaptiveMobile Security Ltd can confirm, as a result of in-depth threat analysis on U.S. cellular networks that the U.S. is under continuous and consistent attack from other Nation-States attempting to surveil key U.S. personnel, and abuse data privacy/sovereignty of U.S. cellular subscribers.

AdaptiveMobile Security Ltd.

Most mobile networks contain a unified management system (also referred to as Operational Support System [OSS]) that is used to control and provision network elements in the entire network. These systems require operators to open a remote direct connection from an external network. As with any application, these management systems might contain security vulnerabilities that will allow an attacker to escalate access and pivot attacks to the rest of the network. The challenge to the attacker is that OSS systems and their implementations are unique to each vendor and an attack might not scale across vendor products.

---

[105] M. Szczys, Poking at the femtocell hardware in an AT&T Microcell, 2012; Kevin Redon SECT, Technical University of Berlin, Hacking Femtocells a femtostep to the holy grail, 2010; T. H. Choice, The Vodafone Access Gateway / UMTS Femto cell / Vodafone Sure Signal, thc.org, 2011.

[106] J. Finkle, Researchers hack Verizon device, turn it into mobile spy station, New York: Reuters, 2013.

[107] http://cgi.di.uoa.gr/~xenakis/Published/53-COSE-2014/Attacking%20the%20HLR%20of%203G%20Networks.pdf

Signaling System 7 (SS7). SS7 is a global standard signaling protocol dating back over three decades and is used for telecommunications traffic for most of the world's PSTN calls, including wireline and legacy cellular networks. Significant weaknesses in SS7 have been known for more than a decade and 3GPP first issued a direct warning in 1999 saying, "The problem with the current SS7 system is that messages can be altered, injected or deleted into the global SS7 networks in an uncontrolled manner."[108] SS7 is the historic control plane for mobile networks; although in VoIP networks, including LTE, it has been supplanted by the Diameter Protocol. Most networks use both protocols and it is common for SS7 messages to be "translated" into their Diameter equivalent.

Gaining unauthorized access to the core SS7 or Diameter network is a risk since there are tens of thousands of entry points worldwide, many of which are controlled by countries or organizations that support terrorism or espionage. Today, networks based on SS7 protocols manage the circuit-switched links among hundreds of carriers for wireline and wireless services and operators serving the majority of mobile subscribers worldwide. SS7 is used worldwide to route phone calls as well as SMS text messages.

A number of threats against SS7 have been publicly described, including the ability to determine the physical location of cellular mobile devices, disrupt phone service from individual phones to entire networks, intercept or block SMS text messages, and redirect or eavesdrop on voice conversations.[109] Threats against SS7 were demonstrated in an April 2016 report on 60 Minutes (and rebroadcast in September 2016), and reported previously, including in presentations by German researcher Tobias Engel at the Chaos Communication Congress security conference in Berlin in 2008[110] and again in 2014.[111] Performing these attacks requires access to SS7, which traditionally has been available only to the operators of phone networks. However, in his 2014 presentation, Engel provided several examples of techniques that could be used to obtain SS7 access. These techniques include attacking network operator equipment left unsecured on the Internet, gaining access through femtocells,[112] or simply purchasing access from a phone network operator.

IV.4.5 External Networks

External networks include the historic PSTN or wireline phones, media networks such as those used to make television broadcasts available via cellular networks, and the Internet. Because these services are not part of the core cellular system, they are called "over-the-top" (OTT) services.

These OTT services are increasingly what citizens rely on and access when using their cellular mobile devices. While these can add additional layers of security, they also can be weaknesses in and of themselves. OTT messaging services can offer substantially more default security than historic cellular services such as SMS and Multimedia Messaging Service (MMS) although they

---

[108] 3G TR 33.900 V1.2.0 (2000-01) Technical Specification 3rd Generation Partnership Project; Technical Specification Group SA WG3; A Guide to 3rd Generation Security (3G TR 33.900 version 1.2.0)
[109] https://www.ptsecurity.com/upload/ptcom/PT-SS7-AD-Data-Sheet-eng.pdf
[110] https://www.youtube.com/watch?v=q0n5ySqbfdI
[111] https://berlin.ccc.de/~tobias/31c3-ss7-locate-track-manipulate.pdf
[112] A small, low-power cellular base station, typically designed for use in a home or small business

do vary widely in their default level of security. Many offer no enhancement at all while others use privacy and security as a key differentiator to attract users.

IV.4.6 Defenses

Because cellular networks are so complex, with each generation or type having similar, yet unique components, software, hardware, firmware, and implementations, defenses also are complex and must be implemented at many layers. For some threats, each type of device in the network needs specific protection mechanisms. Based on published reports, these mechanisms are rarely implemented in most carrier networks and in fact 35 percent of recently surveyed mobile network operators reported that "they did not know" if they had experienced a security incident on the packet core that led to a customer-visible outage.[113]

Of the three most common threats against mobile networks only the first has an effective defense, the second is partially mitigated, and the third (geolocation) has no defense:

- Threats of illegal eavesdropping, data manipulation, and data theft can be mitigated to a degree with secure storage on endpoints and use of encryption for communications in transit. Increasingly, mobile operating systems offer services that can help to mitigate these threats, although some of these services may create other issues for network defenders and breach investigators. Failure to secure sensitive information—whether for personal or professional use—can have serious consequences, and both enterprises and users need to be aware of the benefits and challenges of using protection technologies.

- DoS attacks against individual mobile phones, types of phones, cellular towers, regions or entire service providers are possible. Although the entire industry works extremely hard to eliminate or reduce this threat, it should always be assumed that advanced attackers can execute denial of service attacks at any level. For this reason, any critical communication elements should have an alternative method for use in emergencies— whether personal, regional, or national—no matter if the cause is manmade or natural.

- Geolocation is so innate to basic cellular network operations and so pervasive in mobile application-based services, it is virtually impossible to protect. It can be hardened and its attack surface (e.g., for device and identity tracking) can be reduced, but this will take a sustained effort and may never be successful. It should always be assumed that if a mobile phone is powered on it can be geolocated by a skilled attacker.

Mobile application developers should be encouraged to use the network security features provided by the Android and iOS operating systems to protect the network traffic of their applications against interception or manipulation.

Mobile operating systems are evolving to strongly encourage application developers to treat the network as untrusted and encrypt all network communication at the application level. iOS 9 introduced the App Transport Security feature, which by default requires new mobile applications to use TLS to secure all network communication, unless the app developer explicitly opts out. Android 6 similarly introduced a "uses cleartext traffic" declaration, which has evolved in Android 7 into the new Network Security Configuration feature to help app developers avoid

---

[113] http://pages.arbornetworks.com/rs/arbor/images/WISR2014_EN2014.pdf

many common network security mistakes.[114] To mitigate installation of malicious certificates on cellular mobile devices, beginning with Android 7 the default behavior for applications is to ignore root certificate authorities (also known as trust anchors) added to the device's trust store by the device user or by an enterprise administrator. Instead, applications by default will only trust the root certificate authorities bundled with the operating system. Nick Kralevich of Google's Android Security Team described the potential of nation-state attacks as a motivating factor, specifically referring to a plan under consideration by Kazakhstan to attempt to intercept encrypted network communication.[115]

As another layer of defense, VPNs can be used to route all network traffic through an encrypted tunnel between the cellular mobile device and an enterprise-controlled network. A VPN would automatically protect all network traffic from eavesdropping or manipulation, even if inadvertently sent insecurely at the application level. However, VPNs introduce network performance and battery life issues due to the extra overhead and are vulnerable to sophisticated attacks. They may also introduce privacy concerns in BYOD environments where personally owned devices are being used to access enterprise resources as well as for sensitive personal activities (e.g., health care or online banking).

For protection against SS7 attacks, RFI respondent Adaptive Mobile referred to the SS7 Interconnect Security Monitoring Guidelines (GSMA FS.11) published by the GSM Alliance as well as their own products and services designed for use by mobile carriers.

Table 4 summarizes available defenses against mobile networks and their ability to protect (prevent), detect, or respond to those threats.

Table 4. Available Defenses to Mitigate Attacks on Mobile Networks

Defense	Description	Protect	Detect	Respond
Ensure devices use end-to-end encryption for all communications paths	Due to the nature of carrier networks no voice or data should depend solely on the network for confidentiality or integrity protection.	*		
DoS, DDoS attacks against network	Dozens of attack types exist, so listing each is impossible as is determining the ability to protect against, detect, or respond to the specific attack type because this is highly dependent on carrier network implementation and defenses.			

IV.4.7 Summary of Gaps in Mobile Network Defenses

As described in the previous sections, there are gaps in mobile network protections including:

- Each network component of carrier infrastructure needs specific protection mechanisms, which appear to be rarely implemented by carriers per published reports.[116]

---

[114] Android Best Practices for Security and Privacy at developer.android.com
[115] https://www.blackhat.com/docs/us-16/materials/us-16-Kralevich-The-Art-Of-Defense-How-Vulnerabilities-Help-Shape-Security-Features-And-Mitigations-In-Android.pdf
[116] http://pages.arbornetworks.com/rs/arbor/images/WISR2014_EN2014.pdf; http://ss7map.p1sec.com/country/United%20States/

- Limited or no ability to protect against geolocation of mobile devices and their users.
- The only reliable mitigation against DoS attacks on cellular towers, regions or service providers is alternate communication methods for emergencies due to the large number of known and unmitigated attacks available against network infrastructure.
- Inability to determine whether U.S. carriers have implemented GSMA Interconnect Security Monitoring Guidelines for protection against SS7 attacks.[117]
- SS7 attack types can be used to target key U.S. Federal Government personnel both in the United States and traveling or working overseas. U.S. carriers have established direct roaming partners that include foreign carriers based in China, Iran, Lebanon, Myanmar, Russia, Syria, Sudan, Vietnam, and Zimbabwe—all of which may actively seek to track, intercept, or attack mobile devices associated with U.S. Federal Government personnel. Government use of mobile devices overseas should be informed by threat intelligence and emerging attacker tactics, techniques, and procedures.

IV.4.8 Public Safety Networks

FirstNet Nationwide Public Safety Broadband Network (NPSBN). Signed into law on February 22, 2012, the Middle Class Tax Relief and Job Creation Act created the First Responder Network Authority (FirstNet). The law gives FirstNet the mission to ensure the building, operation and maintenance of the first high-speed, nationwide wireless broadband network dedicated to public safety. The FirstNet network will provide an interoperable broadband data network for emergency and day to day public safety communications. As of this writing, FirstNet is completing a comprehensive federal acquisition process for a private sector partner to deploy the network across the United States using FirstNet's nationwide spectrum license.

FirstNet will be a public safety network built to meet the needs of the nation's first responders, including law enforcement, firefighters, paramedics and other public-safety officials. Qualified federal users may consider using mobile services from FirstNet. FirstNet is in the Request for Proposal (RFP) process as this report is being written. FirstNet issued detailed security solution concepts in Appendix J-10 of its public RFP.[118] At this point, these are security concepts and objectives but not thresholds. However, it is likely that it will be based on work completed by NIST on LTE security vulnerabilities and hardening and the final solution will be deployed following these guidelines.

Next Generation 911 (NG911) Services. 911 services typically operate over standard voice-based telephone networks and use software such as computer-aided dispatch systems that operate on closed, internal networks with little to no interconnections with other systems. The limited means of entry into the traditional 911 network limited potential attack vectors and what little cyber-risk existed could be managed easily. NG911's interconnections enable new response capabilities, including data (e.g., video, text) receipt from the public over a variety of networks, data-sharing between public safety answering points (PSAP), improved location data, and enhanced survivability through the establishment of virtual PSAPs. However, they also represent new vectors for attack that can disrupt or disable PSAP operations. Cyber-risks do present a new

---

[117] Ibid.
[118] https://www.fbo.gov/utils/view?id=7d9982dba8e87f697802f846f08601b8

56

level of exposure that PSAPs must understand and actively manage as a part of operations. As cyber threats grow in complexity and sophistication, attacks against an NG911 system could occur with greater automation from a broader geographic area. Once risks are identified and protection mitigations are in place, the NG911 community can focus on detection and advance planning.[119]

An example of a threat area that has drawn the concern of Government regulators is 911 emergency services robocalling and caller ID spoofing. PSAPS have received 911 emergency calls without caller IDs. These calls could be legitimate or could be spoofed emergency calls originating from anywhere in the world.[120] VoIP interconnects are often the culprit because they allow access to the PSTN without enforcing security controls needed to ensure a caller ID is present and not spoofed. The caller may then give the PSAP operator a false address causing first responders to be called to a nonexistent emergency, possibly depriving a real emergency caller of lifesaving service. Public safety concerns are beginning to address this problem through additional security standards and best practices, however, the ultimate solution is to use digital certificates and mutual authentication on all VoIP systems to prevent identity spoofing.

IV.5 Device Physical Access

The small, portable nature of mobile devices increases their susceptibility to physical-based threats. Some of these threats are shown in Figure 14.

---

[119] https://www.dhs.gov/sites/default/files/publications/NG911%20Cybersecurity%20Primer%20041816%20-%20508%20compliant.pdf
[120] http://arstechnica.com/tech-policy/2009/02/911-service-not-prepared-for-new-generation-of-pranksters/

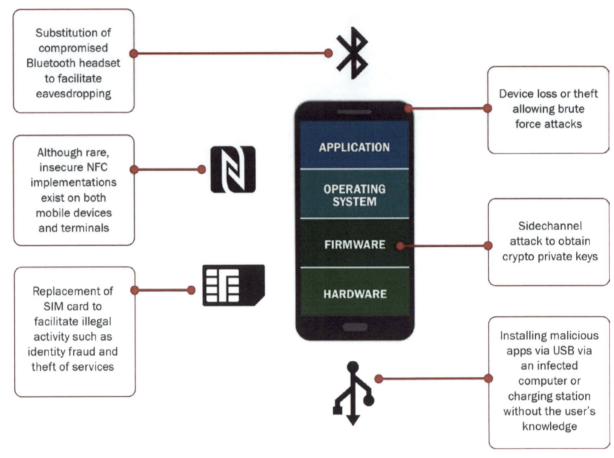

Figure 14. Threats from Physical Access to Device

IV.5.1 Threats

According to a *Consumer Reports* survey, 2.1 million mobile phones were stolen from Americans in 2014 and 3.1 million were lost.[121] Mobile device users may also temporarily give up possession of their devices at locations such as international border crossings. Depending on the configuration of these devices, data stored on the device potentially could be obtained, accessed, or modified along with data stored on network-based enterprise resources or other online resources (e.g., online banking) accessed from the mobile device. Skycure's first quarter 2016 Mobile Threat Intelligence Report found that 31 percent of mobile devices do not have a lock screen passcode, the first line of defense against physical attacks.[122] NowSecure also found in its 2016 Mobile Security Report that "43 percent of mobile users do not use a passcode, Personal Identification Number (PIN), or pattern lock on their device."[123]

The recent addition of fingerprint sensors to many mobile devices has encouraged users to set a screen lock passcode since having a passcode is required for enabling the fingerprint sensor. Adrian Ludwig of Google's Android Security Team reported that the use of the lock screen has

---

[121] http://www.consumerreports.org/cro/news/2015/06/smartphone-thefts-on-the-decline/index.htm
[122] https://www.skycure.com/wp-content/uploads/2016/06/Skycure-Q1-2016-MobileThreatIntelligenceReport.pdf
[123] https://info.nowsecure.com/rs/201-XEW-873/images/2016-NowSecure-mobile-security-report.pdf

increased from around 50 percent to 90 percent on Android devices with a fingerprint sensor.[124] Apple's Touch ID has likely had similar effects on iOS devices.

Apple and Google have added activation lock capabilities to their mobile devices that prevent lost or stolen devices from being factory reset, lowering the economic incentives for criminals to steal devices. The referenced *Consumer Reports* survey notes that the rate of mobile phone thefts declined from 2013 (3.1 million phones) to 2014 (2.1 million phones) possibly because of the inclusion of activation lock capabilities in Apple devices (they had not been adopted by Android devices at the time).

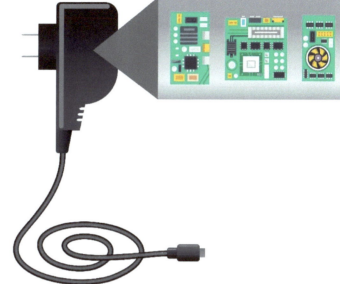

Other physical-based attack vectors against mobile devices exist. Mobile devices use USB (or a similar communication channel such as Apple's Lightning) primarily for power charging, but the same interface enables data communication to and from a mobile device. If a mobile device is plugged in to a compromised or malicious PC or charging station the PC or charging station could potentially abuse the communication channel to attempt to exploit vulnerabilities on the mobile device or to steal sensitive data. Billy Lau et al. of Georgia Tech demonstrated a proof-of-concept of this kind of attack against iOS devices in 2013[125] and in March 2016 Palo Alto Networks

Figure 15. USB Charger with Modified Circuit Board

reported on a family of malware they named "AceDeceiver" that attacks iOS devices from compromised Windows PCs.[126] Figure 15 is an example of a USB charger, which is typically modified by inserting an extremely small PC board with a single chip computer on it capable of advanced pre-programmed attacks.

To combat USB attacks, iOS and Android devices now require the mobile device user to explicitly trust any new PC to which the device has not previously connected. The device screen must be unlocked to establish the trust.

Also, the USB communication channel could potentially be abused in the reverse direction, enabling a compromised mobile device to launch attacks against the host device to which it is connected. The USB protocol can, for example, be abused to enable the mobile device to impersonate a keyboard, mouse, or storage device for a PC and perform arbitrary actions. The potential for this form of attack was described by Angelos Stavrou et al. in 2010.[127] Android

---

[124] https://www.youtube.com/watch?v=XZzLjllizYs (14 minutes in)
[125] https://media.blackhat.com/us-13/US-13-Lau-Mactans-Injecting-Malware-into-iOS-Devices-via-Malicious-Chargers-WP.pdf
[126] http://researchcenter.paloaltonetworks.com/2016/03/acedeceiver-first-ios-trojan-exploiting-apple-drm-design-flaws-to-infect-any-ios-device/
[127] http://cs.gmu.edu/~astavrou/research/acsac10.pdf

devices also have spread malware to host systems. This malware has been discovered in the USB charging ports in aircraft cabins.[128]

IV.5.2 Defenses

The most important action to defend against physical threats is to ensure that mobile devices always have a screen lock PIN or password. If there is not a screen lock, it is easy for an attacker to access the data or functionality of a lost or stolen mobile device. Enrolling devices into an EMM system provides an enterprise the ability to enforce use of a screen lock.

Enterprise capabilities should be put in place to remotely track and—when necessary—remotely wipe mobile devices. These capabilities can be provided by EMM systems, by the device or OS vendor, or by third-party mobile security vendors. On iOS devices, Apple's Device Enrollment Program can be used to automatically enroll enterprise-owned devices into enterprise management and ensure the devices cannot be removed from management.

Users should be advised not to plug mobile devices directly into public USB charging ports unless a charge-only adapter or cable is used. They should instead carry and use their own charging devices.

Table 5 summarizes available defenses against physical attacks to devices and their ability to protect (prevent), detect, or respond to those threats.

Table 5. Available Defenses to Mitigate Physical Attacks

Defense	Description	Protect	Detect	Respond
Ensure devices are enterprise-managed	Ensure devices are managed by an EMM/MDM solution, enabling the ability to enforce security policies, monitor device state as well as remotely track or wipe lost or stolen devices.	*	*	*
Ensure device screen lock is enabled	Use an EMM/MDM solution to enforce policies on mobile devices to ensure the device screen lock is enabled with an appropriately strong password.	*		

IV.5.3 Summary of Gaps in Device Physical Access Defenses

The mobile technology industry has taken concrete steps toward defenses for physical threats, but gaps remain, including:

- Despite the industry's efforts to encourage use of device screen lock capabilities, there is still more work to be done to encourage users to use screen lock on their devices.
- Device vendors have taken steps to prevent USB-based attacks against mobile devices from compromised PCs or malicious charging stations. However, more work is needed to defend against attacks in the opposite direction: from a mobile device to a PC.
- Existing strong authentication solutions are not designed to complement the mobile form factor. More research is needed to incorporate the unique sensor data (motion sensor/

---

[128] http://www.reuters.com/article/us-nuclearpower-cyber-germany-idUSKCN0XN2OS

accelerometer, gyroscope, GPS, force sensor, capacitive sensor and camera) captured by the device to uniquely identify the registered device user.

IV.6 Mobile Enterprise

The mobile enterprise consists of systems, applications, processes, and people that work together to control, manage, and integrate the use of mobile devices and related technologies into business and mission operations. The mobile enterprise includes the mobile devices themselves and the back-end infrastructure such as the servers used to manage devices and host enterprise application stores. Supporting infrastructure such as email servers, file servers, databases, directory servers, and authentication servers as well as networking infrastructure are parts of the mobile enterprise.

IV.6.1 Enterprise Threats from Mobile Devices

Mobile devices do bring new threats to enterprises and can be used to target enterprise systems. Mobile devices form a unique class of end user equipment that frequently moves inside and outside of enterprise networks.[129] This movement means that mobile devices compromised elsewhere can be used as vectors to compromise other enterprise devices or even the enterprise. This vulnerability has not gone unnoticed by criminals and at least one family of malware specifically employs this weakness, using compromised Android phones to target enterprise systems.[130]

While criminal acts targeting the mobile ecosystem or leveraging it to attack other systems or infrastructure is uncommon in the United States, there are few differences between the cellular system in the United States and in most other countries in the world. In fact, U.S. export of technologies to other countries means there is a large global base for criminals to develop attack techniques that can later be used within U.S. borders. An example of this is automated teller machine (ATM) malware discovered in Mexico three years ago that is affecting U.S. manufactured ATMs; a key component of this malware is the use of a cell phone to trigger the attack via SMS.[131]

In terms of maturity, mobile management is medium mature; mobile security is immature; and dynamic threat management is very immature.

David Jevans, Vice President Mobile Security, Proofpoint

A growing number of incidents are now being reported that document the spread of malware from Android devices to other systems including aircraft flight decks.[132] This may occur because in an attempt to charge Android devices, users (e.g., aircraft crews) plug them into any available USB port, even if they should not. Most Android devices can be mounted as a shared drive in

---

[129] http://blog.trendmicro.com/the-android-malware-problem/
[130] http://blog.trendmicro.com/trendlabs-security-intelligence/dresscode-potential-impact-enterprises/
[131] ATM Malware on the Rise: A Comprehensive Overview of the Digital ATM Threat, Trend Micro Forward-Looking Threat Research (FTR) Team and Europol's European Cybercrime Center (EC3), 2016
[132] http://www.reuters.com/article/us-nuclearpower-cyber-germany-idUSKCN0XN2OS

such an environment. At this time, the malware is designed to target other Android devices, but this is an effective vector for targeting other systems.

IV.6.2 Enterprise Mobility Management

IT administrators rely on EMM technologies to control and manage mobile data, mobile devices, and their connections with enterprise resources. An EMM solution consists of a client agent that resides on the mobile device to receive and implement management commands sent by an administrative server that resides on the premises of the enterprise network or as a cloud-based service. EMMs include an MDM system to lock down the device and provision device-level settings. For instance, a MDM can control VPN configurations or pre-defined Wi-Fi settings to help secure connections between the device and enterprise resources. Additional MDM services include enforcing compliance with device security policies, remote wiping, remote locking, and blocking the installation of unauthorized apps.

EMMs may also include MAM to control and secure specific enterprise apps, leaving personal apps untouched. MAMs can remotely install and uninstall enterprise apps, manage the mobile app inventory, ensure apps on mobile devices are up to date, and selectively wipe and encrypt enterprise app data. MAMs may also integrate with internal and/or external app stores and third-party app security services.

Some EMM solutions also offer specialized apps for secure web browsing and reading corporate email, and separating business apps from personal apps. The central, critical role EMMs play in the management and security of all aspects of enterprise mobility can make them targets for exploitation by attackers. Some of these attacks are shown in Figure 16.

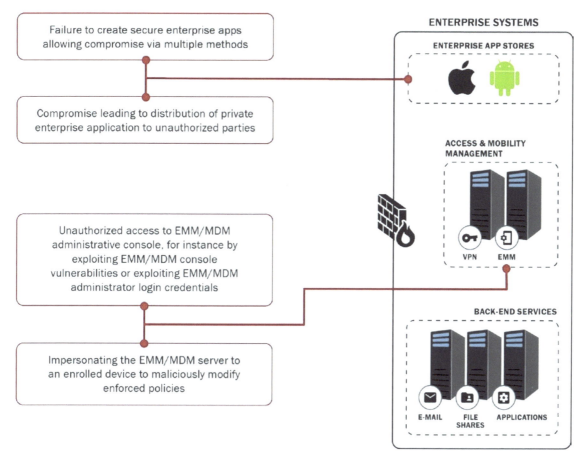

Figure 16. Threats to the Mobile Enterprise

IV.6.2.1   Threats

Because EMM systems have elevated privileges, intruders can leverage control over EMMs to launch attacks against mobile devices and the mobile enterprise. An attacker may steal administrative credentials or exploit vulnerabilities in the EMM infrastructure or software to gain unauthorized access to the administrative console and launch attacks against mobile devices. For example, compromise of the EMM management console could allow an attacker to push malicious applications, send rogue root certificates, or change policies and configuration settings to many managed mobile devices at once.[133] These changes can leave mobile devices susceptible to additional exploitation by an attacker.

If an attacker can compromise the security of the interactions between the EMM and the mobile devices under its control, he or she potentially gains the ability to conduct several kinds of attacks against the enterprise. A successful man-in-the-middle attack between an EMM and a device potentially enables an attacker to send incorrect location or status messages or impede the sending of such information. Follow-on effects of such actions could include preventing a device owner from being able to locate a stolen device, preventing the organization from discovering that a device has been compromised, or giving the false impression that organizational policies

---

[133] http://www.wired.co.uk/article/samsung-knox-security-vulnerabilities

are being enforced on the device. Such an attack might also be used to falsely send data that indicates that the device has received all security updates when it has not.

Direct attacks on an EMM could include DoS attacks designed to cripple the ability of mobile workers to retrieve documents or data or to provide data to the enterprise. Subtler attacks may include exploiting the EMM to gain access to enterprise data or to replace documents and data with incorrect or malicious versions. A compromise of the EMM infrastructure also could be used as a point from which an attacker pivots to enumerate or attack other enterprise infrastructure such as certificate authorities, databases, directory servers, and application servers.

An attacker also could bypass the resident EMM agent by exploiting vulnerabilities in the operating system to gain a foothold on the device, which the agent may not be able to monitor or detect.[134] Moreover, the attacker could bypass encryption, secure containers, or other security measures provided by the EMM agent and compromise enterprise data on the mobile device. Table 6 summarizes the threats to EMMs and the potential impacts of attacks on these systems.

Table 6. Enterprise Mobility Management Threats and Impact

EMM Threat	Impact
Unauthorized access to EMM administrative console Impersonation of EMM server	• Infect or inhibit normal operation of EMM system • Unauthorized wiping of data from device • Force device misconfigurations to facilitate further attacks • Force malicious app download to mobile device to facilitate further attacks • Track user behavior, device location, call logs, text messages, personal contacts, etc.
Bypass or subvert EMM agent on mobile device	• Alter, delete, steal enterprise data transferred or managed by the MDM agent • Infect, inhibit normal operation of EMM agent

IV.6.2.2 Defenses

Given the EMM infrastructure's integration with and reliance on other enterprise systems, measures should be implemented to protect and monitor these systems. Some of the same defenses that are used to protect other enterprise IT infrastructure are equally applicable to protecting EMM/MDM systems. For example, man-in-the-middle attacks can be prevented through use of digital certificates and mutual authentication of devices and EMM servers. Mutual authentication between all components of the EMM and any supporting infrastructure (databases, directory servers, etc.), can provide assurance that each side of the communication is authentic. It is also imperative that communications among key components of the mobile enterprise be protected with strong cryptography and key management.

Network monitoring technologies can be used to detect efforts to perform known or potentially malicious network-based attacks against EMM components or supporting infrastructure (e.g., replay attacks) while web-application firewalls might be used to secure web-based components.

---

[134] http://searchmobilecomputing.techtarget.com/tip/Are-MDM-tools-as-secure-as-you-think; http://www.hypori.com/single-post/2016/06/16/Secure-Enterprise-Mobility-when-MDM-is-an-Attack-Vector; https://www.rsaconference.com/writable/presentations/file_upload/mbs-r02-practical-attacks-against-mdm-solutions-v2.pdf

Out-of-band configuration management and verification techniques and technologies can be used to protect EMM systems and to detect potential violations of the integrity of these systems. Network monitoring and deep-packet inspection solutions, combined with Security Information and Event Management (SIEM) solutions could be used to help detect attempts to exfiltrate documents and data, while digital rights management solutions and encryption solutions can be used to add protection to sensitive documents in the event exfiltration attempts are successful.

RFI respondents identified several products that can detect and respond to attacks against EMM agents on the mobile device. These products focused on behavioral, contextual, and integrity monitoring of the mobile device, its apps, its network activity, and the user. These approaches enable the detection of suspicious or malicious activity such as changes to the EMM agent, rooting of the device, or installation of unverified certificates that could compromise the integrity of the SSL connection to the EMM backend. Some solutions leverage the data feeds from the on-device monitoring service and correlate with other monitoring feeds from the EMM/MDM backend infrastructure for additional analytics.

Other solutions on the device include a TEE, a protected processing environment within which the EMM agent can run. A TEE provides mobile operating system boot integrity, secure storage, device identification, isolated execution, and device authentication capabilities. An EMM agent can exercise these capabilities to isolate itself and still function in the presence of other malicious activity on a device. Responses to malicious activity on a device typically include denying access until the threat is removed. More sophisticated responses are usually facilitated with the help of an EMM system.

There are also products that focus on securing the backend of the EMM system using ephemeral cloud services. A cloud-based network is generated from virtual servers on multiple cloud providers and network components can be changed at random intervals or if under attack. Access to this network is controlled by Public Key Infrastructure (PKI) verified points of entry that can be activated on a scheduled or ad-hoc basis. Hosting the EMM backend in an ephemeral network could limit the persistence of successful attacks and allows the EMM to recover when its network components are changed.

There are many products available to defend EMMs, including monitoring mobile device and mobile enterprise activities for malicious behavior, strong mutual authentication schemes, TEEs, and ephemeral networks, however, integration of multiple defensive products is needed to address all mobile device platforms and provide holistic protection of the EMM system.

Table 7 summarizes available defenses against attacks on EMM systems and indicates their ability to detect, respond to, or recover from those threats.

Table 7. Available Defenses to Mitigate Attacks Against EMM Systems

What	Description	Detect	Respond	Recover

What	Description	Detect	Respond	Recover
Enterprise security audit	Track and log administrative activities, device enrollment events, network activities, etc. of EMM systems. Assure the CDM Phase 1 capabilities for hardware and software asset management (HWAM & SWAM) as well as hardening criteria associated with Configuration Settings Management (CSM) and vulnerability management (VUL) can be identified and reported.	*		
Mobile device security audit	App that runs on the mobile device to monitor the OS, apps, and network connections to identify malicious behavior. This includes monitoring of the EMM agent.	*		
Threat intelligence	Consolidate and correlate security audit feeds from the EMM/MDM mobile device agent and enterprise systems to identify suspicious and malicious behavior.	*	*	
Granular authorization	Support multiple levels of permission or role-based administrative access to enforce the principle of least privilege.	*	*	
Identification and Authentication	Support two-factor authentication for administrative access; integrate with enterprise single-sign-on infrastructure; Open Authorization (OAuth) security mechanisms. Assure that the CDM Phase 2 capabilities for user attributes can be identified and reported.	*		
Secure network connections	Secure communication channels between all components of EMM/MDM, e.g., VPNs, message replay detection and prevention, secure out-of-band messaging channels, etc.	*		
Trusted Execution Environment	Leverage Trust Zone or similar hardware isolation to provide trusted mobile environment (e.g., secure storage) within which the EMM/MDM agent can operate.	*		

IV.6.3 Enterprise Mobile Application Stores

Rather than rely on consumer-oriented app stores, enterprises may operate their own private mobile application stores to manage and distribute mobile applications. Whether custom-built, third-party, or public apps, a private enterprise app store can and should rigorously vet and maintain apps throughout their lifecycle to sanction and secure mobile apps for users.

IV.6.3.1 Threats

Since mobile application stores are the primary method for distributing apps, they have become one of the main attack vectors for infecting mobile devices with malware to facilitate further attacks (Section IV.3.2). Private enterprise app stores also are at risk of distributing malicious apps. Attackers can target administrative credentials, developer credentials, or distribution certificates to distribute mobile malware to victims. Table 8 summarizes the threats facing enterprise mobile app stores and their impact.

Table 8. Threats to Enterprise Mobile App Stores and Corresponding Impact

Mobile Application Store Threat	Impact
Impersonation or unauthorized use of administrator credentials, app developer credentials, or distribution certificates. Bypass or subvert application security analysis or vetting techniques.	• Distribution of private enterprise application to unauthorized parties • Bring app store offline • Modify, replace, or remove an already-deployed app to facilitate further attacks • Distribute malicious app to facilitate further attacks

IV.6.3.2 Defenses

A straightforward approach to protecting an enterprise app store is to require two-factor authentication, employ the principle of least privilege for administrative access, and monitor the infrastructure for unauthorized or malicious behavior.

One available product offers cloud-based backend services that provides a set of APIs for specifying authentication methods for accessing enterprise resources. App developers can require and call these APIs from within their apps to grant enterprise access. Malicious apps that may have subverted vetting would be readily identifiable and denied access if missing the prescribed authentication method and credentials. Other defenses prevent apps from being added without administrator intervention or through a protected (authenticated) API. Several product solutions need to be integrated to protect app stores that deliver apps to different platforms.

Table 9 summarizes defenses to mitigate attacks on enterprise mobile app stores and indicates each defense's ability to detect, respond, or recover from those threats.

Table 9. Available Defenses to Mitigate Attacks Against Enterprise Mobile App Stores

Defense	Description	Detect	Response	Recover
Enterprise security audit	Track and log network and administrative activities associated with app store console.	*		
Mobile device security audit	Conduct on-device monitoring to prevent installation of untrusted developer certificates used by fake apps outside the enterprise app store. Assure that CDM capabilities regarding certificate attributes can be identified and reported.	*		
Threat intelligence	Consolidate and correlate security audit feeds to identify suspicious and malicious behavior.	*	*	
Granular authorization	Implement role-based access controls corresponding to steps in app lifecycle, e.g., split roles for app development and publishing process.	*	*	
Identification and Authentication	Support two-factor authentication for administrative access; integrate with enterprise single-sign-on infrastructure; OAuth security mechanisms; encrypt admin credentials. Assure that CDM Phase 2 capabilities for user attributes can be identified and reported.	*		

IV.6.4 Summary of Gaps in Mobile Enterprise Defenses

There are many products available today that seek to address the threats facing the mobile enterprise. Adaptation of traditional IT enterprise defense solutions to the mobile environment are evolving, but are not mature. Thus, gaps still exist in the ability to respond to attacks against the enterprise, including:

- Limited ability of enterprise mobility products to detect sophisticated attacks against mobile devices.
- Limited ability of EMM solutions to identify vulnerable mobile devices.
- Most EMMs lack the ability to directly update the mobile OS.
- Apple's Device Enrollment Program and similar programs such as Samsung's Knox Mobile Enrollment provide capabilities to ensure enterprise-owned mobile devices are kept under enterprise management control. More work is needed to encourage enterprise adoption of these capabilities.
- Lack of guidance on how to integrate EMM solutions with other enterprise security systems to enable effective response and recovery capabilities to compromised or out-of-compliance mobile devices.
- Improvements in integration of EMM solutions with mobile threat intelligence services.
- Immature vulnerability management processes for mobile OS and mobile apps.
- Stronger mechanisms for data security and data authorization decisions need to be developed. Sensor data could be integrated into authorization decisions thereby providing more granular access control to selected data types based on assurance conditions.

While availability of TEE functionality is growing, the lack of standards for interfacing with it has limited use of the technology. Because it lacks defense mechanisms for running in an environment that can guarantee integrity and confidentially, any device-based defense (e.g., on-device monitoring software, EMM agent) is susceptible to attack. In any case, most solutions only provide detection capabilities, leaving a need for response and recovery capabilities. Moreover, no single approach addresses the entire mobile enterprise and multiple solutions need to be integrated to provide holistic protection. Due to the varying support for different mobile platforms and vendor-specific implementations, integration of the different solutions would be a nontrivial task.

IV.7 Emerging Threats

The study group has also identified several probable emerging threats. These are based on past trends in mobile security, the general evolution of cellular networks, and advances in security research in the public sector, combined with an extensive review of academic security papers. These threats fall into the following categories:

- Open Source Signals Intelligence
- Advances in decryption of cellular network authentication and privacy standards in the public sector
- Advances in "IMSI Catcher" capabilities
- Increasingly sophisticated cybercrime and fraud targeting individuals and corporations
- Increasing use of broad spectrum jamming by citizens seeking privacy

Open Source Signals Intelligence. Public sector advances in intercepting RF based communications as well as analyzing and decrypting them have now coalesced into the field of Open Source Signals Intelligence. This should not be confused with Open Source Intelligence,[135] which is now a widely accepted field used by law enforcement and intelligence agencies around the world. Unfortunately, much of the software and protocols used in RF devices are insecure. At the time of creation (the 1990s) it was assumed that no one, excluding nation states, would have the resources and capability to attack such systems. To maintain backward compatibility, these systems continue to proliferate. The ability to run RF frequency spectrum analyzers, firmware extraction and analysis tools, and protocol analyzers is now within reach of high school students, not just organized crime or nation state intelligence organizations.

Open Source Signals Intelligence is a rapidly expanding and advancing field driven by a number of factors including many rapidly advancing open source software libraries[136] and a growing segment of the American public influenced by popular television shows.[137] At the most advanced level are private sector security firms funded by nation states that directly target cellular systems, smartphones and other mobile devices.[138] In the mid-range are developers of new and existing systems that either mistakenly leave source code and documentation on the Internet or intentionally do so as whistleblowers, enabling penetration of the affected systems.[139] Finally, there is a growing hobbyist or "grey hat" hacker movement interested in unlocking hidden features of devices,[140] as well as intercepting, analyzing and decrypting the communications protocols of common RF devices.[141] Portable phones,[142] key fobs,[143] remote controls,[144] consumer alarm systems,[145] and Wi-Fi gear[146] are targets.

All of this means there is now an increasing number of people who have the skills, time, tools and techniques to attack mobile devices and the underlying networks on which they depend. For this reason, it is likely the activities discussed in this section will increase in the near term.

Decryption of 3G/UMTS Cellular Network Traffic. Publicly available exploits of UMTS (3G) are considered inevitable for the purposes of this report. It has now been over a decade since the first weaknesses were revealed in these standards[147] and since then additional weaknesses have been discovered and made public.[148] Although 3GPP and GSMA have deprecated some security authentication and encryption standards in the past,[149] advances in deploying replacement

---

[135] https://en.wikipedia.org/wiki/Open-source_intelligence
[136] https://en.wikipedia.org/wiki/GNU_Radio; https://en.wikipedia.org/wiki/Ophcrack; https://en.wikipedia.org/wiki/Hashcat; https://en.wikipedia.org/wiki/OsmocomBB; https://en.wikipedia.org/wiki/Aircrack-ng; https://en.wikipedia.org/wiki/OpenBTS
[137] http://arstechnica.com/the-multiverse/2016/09/yes-you-can-hack-cell-phones-like-on-mr-robot-just-not-the-way-they-did/
[138] https://www.wired.com/2016/08/hacking-group-selling-ios-vulnerabilities-state-actors/
[139] https://www.sans.org/reading-room/whitepapers/awareness/data-leakage-threats-mitigation-1931
[140] http://www.newyorker.com/tech/elements/a-short-history-of-hack
[141] https://www.blackhat.com/docs/asia-15/materials/asia-15-Seeber-Hacking-the-Wireless-World-With-Software-Defined-Radio-2.0.pdf
[142] http://securityweekly.com/2009/07/06/sniffing-dect-the-dedectedorg/
[143] https://www.wired.com/2014/08/wireless-car-hack/
[144] http://v3gard.com/2014/12/hacking-garage-door-remote-controllers/
[145] http://boredhackerblog.blogspot.com/2016/02/how-we-broke-into-your-house.html
[146] http://www.computerworld.com/article/2913356/cybercrime-hacking/2-more-wireless-baby-monitors-hacked-hackers-remotely-spied-on-babies-and-parents.html
[147] http://www.cs.technion.ac.il/users/wwwb/cgi-bin/tr-get.cgi/2006/CS/CS-2006-07.pdf
[148] http://eprint.iacr.org/2010/013
[149] https://en.wikipedia.org/wiki/A5/2

systems may not be keeping pace with attacks on the systems currently in use and currently no deprecation schedule is in place if the UMTS (3G) UEA1/UIA1 security algorithms fall.

The rise of crypto currencies has fueled a market in high-speed encryption systems. In the past most brute force attacks on encryption standards ran directly on standard central processing units (CPUs) and were available only to nation states. The explosion of crypto currencies has advanced this field first to graphics processing unit (GPU)-based crypto to field-programmable gate arrays (FPGA) and finally to custom application-specific integrated circuits (ASICs), which can perform cryptographic calculations several orders of magnitude faster than the CPU-based systems used in the past. ASIC based systems are also increasing in speed much faster than Moore's Law and businesses selling encryption as a service are spreading.[150] These are now widely available and pose a considerable risk to mobile device privacy and security.

"IMSI Catchers" and Passive Cellular Interceptors. IMSI catchers (or rogue base stations) and passive cellular interceptors are a growing threat because they allow hackers, criminals, and spies to track cell phone users and monitor or record conversations and text messages.[151] They are being marketed worldwide for 2G, 3G, and 4G exploitation. Passive cellular interceptors are difficult to detect since they only listen.[152] Even low-cost LTE interception units have been advertised to perform tracking.[153] Hackers and attackers alike now commonly use these on GSM, UMTS, CDMA2000, and LTE networks and they were a focus of many recent hacker conferences.[154] It should be anticipated that software based open source versions of these tools will eventually exceed the capabilities of commercial units just as protocol decoders have done in the last decade.[155]

Cybercrime and Fraud. Because the global mobile ecosystem is so large and so much money exchanges hands, criminals will continue to target it. Although carriers continue to deploy new and more advanced fraud detection systems, criminals continue to find ways to defeat these defenses. Unfortunately, several more advanced technologies seem to be emerging from Chinese manufacturers that can counter many of these detection systems. In some cases, they completely bypass MNO networks and operate as "SMS servers" or localized cellular networks. In other cases, the technologies simply reduce the price of committing fraud which lets them operate at lower thresholds and makes them harder to detect.

Jamming. Although private use of jammers is generally illegal,[156] they are also likely to be increasingly used to disrupt cell phone communications. Cell phone jammers are widely available for purchase on the Internet[157] including plans and kits[158] and are even listed by

[150] http://www.economist.com/news/business/21638124-minting-digital-currency-has-become-big-ruthlessly-competitive-business-magic
[151] https://www.schneier.com/blog/archives/2015/04/the_further_dem_1.html
[152] http://blog.se-sy.org/2015/10/lte-attacks-2015.html
[153] http://arstechnica.com/security/2015/10/low-cost-imsi-catcher-for-4glte-networks-track-phones-precise-locations/
[154] https://media.defcon.org/DEF%20CON%2024/DEF%20CON%2024%20presentations/DEFCON-24-Eric-Escobar-Rogue-Cell-Towers-UPDATED.pdf; https://www.blackhat.comhttp://sectools.org/tag/sniffers//docs/eu-15/materials/eu-15-Borgaonkar-LTE-And-IMSI-Catcher-Myths.pdf; https://media.defcon.org/DEF%20CON%2024/DEF%20CON%2024%20presentations/DEFCON-24-Zhang-Shan-Forcing-Targeted-Lte-Cellphone-Into-Unsafe-Network.pdf
[155] https://pdfs.semanticscholar.org/38f0/641fc38868aad84a9008b13769afbc31c3b1.pdf; http://sectools.org/tag/sniffers/
[156] https://www.fcc.gov/general/jamming-cell-phones-and-gps-equipment-against-law
[157] http://www.cell-jammers.com/military-jammers; http://www.thesignaljammer.com/categories/Cell-Phone-Jammers/

range[159] to show how jammers can deny service across large service areas. In addition, jammers can be used to cause cell phones to move off 3G and 4G networks and on to 2G networks where interception and decryption is much easier.[160] The number of incidents in which jammers are being used by individuals to increase their own privacy is rising.[161] As citizens become aware of just how invasive many new technologies are, it is likely that some will turn to jammers to create a personal "privacy bubble". In fact, this selling point is a key marketing tactic driving the sales of jammers.[162] It is likely that the United States will see increases in the number of incidents involving jamming.

IV.8 A Framework for Modeling Mobile Threats

The cybersecurity community has developed a collection of threat models that decompose threats into the tactics and techniques (methods) used by attackers to compromise information and information systems. The primary use of these models is to better understand how an attacker can gain entry to an IT system, then design defenses to protect against the threat, detect it if it occurs, and then respond to, and recover from the incident.

One such defensive threat model is the seven-stage Cyber Attack Lifecycle (first articulated by Lockheed Martin as the Cyber Kill Chain®),[163] which is frequently used to depict the stages of an attack campaign against IT systems. The model spans reconnaissance (e.g., research and selection of targets) through exploit (e.g., installation of malware on the device) to the maintain state (persistence). Ideally, enterprises would protect against or detect attack campaigns early in the lifecycle (i.e., before the exploit stage at the center of Figure 17), prior to the attacker obtaining a foothold in the enterprise network. However, if the attack is successful, enterprises must be able to detect, respond, and recover from the attacker's post-exploit actions.

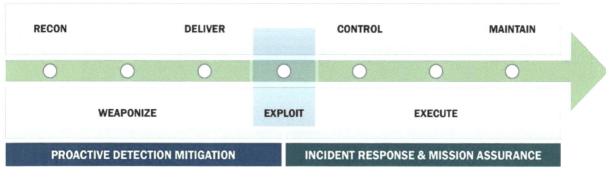

Figure 17: Stages of the Cyber Attack Lifecycle[164]

Appendix E presents a model that decomposes the mobile security threats described in Sections IV.2 through IV.6 into the methods used by attackers to compromise mobile systems by

---

[158] http://hacknmod.com/hack/a-diy-mini-rf-cell-phone-jammer/
[159] http://www.projammers.com/en/mobile-phone-jammers/according-to-range/
[160] http://web2-clone.research.att.com/export/sites/att_labs/techdocs/TD_101153.pdf
[161] https://www.cnet.com/news/truck-driver-has-gps-jammer-accidentally-jams-newark-airport/;
    https://www.cnet.com/news/man-put-cell-phone-jammer-in-car-to-stop-driver-calls-fcc-says/
[162] http://www.jammer-store.com/privavy-protection-with-jammers-which-gadget-can-harm-us-the-most
[163] http://www.lockheedmartin.com/content/dam/lockheed/data/corporate/documents/LM-White-Paper-Intel-Driven-Defense.pdf
[164] https://www.mitre.org/capabilities/cybersecurity/threat-based-defense

expanding the stages of the Cyber Attack Lifecycle into tactic categories and defining publicly observed techniques within those categories that can be used by attackers. While the prior sections described how deliberate or accidental threats can compromise individual elements of the mobile ecosystem, this model focuses on how a deliberate attack is carried out across the mobile ecosystem, then overlays that model with a heat map visualizing defensive coverage and gaps.

V. Threat Prioritization, Study Findings, and Gaps

Threats to the Government's use of mobile devices are real and exist across all elements of the mobile ecosystem. This is evident from the threat assessment conducted for this study and documented in the previous sections. The corresponding analysis of available defenses shows that despite significant advances in addressing both deliberate and accidental threats to mobile security, gaps remain that will command additional effort by Government and industry to reduce the risk of using mobile technologies. This section summarizes the study's findings, highest-priority threats, and gaps in mitigations.

Findings from review and analysis of the draft *Mobile Threat Catalogue*, RFI responses, and one-on-one interviews include threats identified as high-priority, whether due to limitations in or lack of defensive mechanisms or because of the constantly evolving threat landscape and pace of technology change. The findings also include recommendations for enhanced information sharing, implementation of standards and best practices, and the need for the Government to provide industry a unified view of its security objectives and requirements. The study's analysis of threats identified the need for people, process, and technology defenses to address mobile security threats, and highlighted gaps in current policies, processes, and technologies that need to be updated or developed. The following sections summarize the findings; recommendations to address the threats and gaps in defenses are presented in the final sections of this report.

V.1   Threats and Issues Identified by Industry

Top Threats Identified by Industry. During one-on-one interviews with industry, interviewees were asked what they considered to be the top threats to the mobile ecosystem and which areas of the ecosystem they believed were insecure. While responses largely reflect the point of view of a specific area of the ecosystem, there were some commonalities that are summarized below:

- Mobile Applications: Malware (including backdoors, ransomware, and privilege escalation) and vulnerabilities in mobile apps and systems.
- Networks: Rogue cellular base stations and Wi-Fi access points; Man-in-the-Middle attacks on communications.
- Mobile Device Technology Stack: Delays in security updates and zero-day exploits against software and firmware, particularly the baseband.
- Devices: Loss or theft of a mobile device.
- Devices and Applications: Exfiltration or access to sensitive (personal or business) data without user awareness or consent.
- User: Tricking users into visiting malicious links and downloading malware through Phishing, SMiShing, or spoofing.

Issues and Areas of Concern Identified by Industry. Discussion with industry representatives highlighted additional areas of concern and recommendations for Government use of mobile devices:

- Broad adoption and enforcement of cyber security best practices, e.g., use of PIN/password, two-factor authentication, encryption of communications (treat all networks as untrusted), and use of certificate pinning to authenticate endpoints.
- Need for the Federal Government to present a unified view of its security architecture and

increase transparency regarding the Government's security objectives and requirements.

- Inability of the Federal Government to keep pace with the speed of technology change and dynamic threats. The Government needs to be nimble and focus on security goals and performance objectives. Industry noted that agencies tend to focus more on compliance and desire for a specific type of device rather than defining security requirements and allowing industry to develop solutions to meet those requirements.
- Need for user security awareness and training to reinforce and promote good cyber hygiene practices for use of mobile devices and mobile apps.
- Closer Government-industry collaboration on information sharing on vulnerabilities and threat intelligence.
- Need for enhanced U.S. Government representation in international SDOs to define next-generation network standards such as fifth generation mobile networks and self-organizing networks.

Summary Observations—RFI Responses on Standards and Best Practices. Following are observations of note from RFI respondents regarding SDOs and standards:

- In addition to the standards described in Section III.2, there are other standards and industry practices for everything from how to design an EMM solution to how to develop good software. The list of standards and best practices championed by industry, academia and the research community, and governments is extensive.
- SDOs ultimately all have the same basic objective: to provide the best, most-cost effective security for mobile technologies individually and for the ecosystem in aggregate.
- Although there is some overlap in membership across these SDOs, in many cases each operates independently. This leads to situations in which the efforts are disjointed and sometimes at odds with each other.
- Several of the companies consulted for this report indicated their strong desire for Government involvement in and insight on the development of standards and best practices. In an environment of competing priorities and approaches, some in industry believe the U.S. Government can play a role to harmonize and guide the evolution and adoption of standards. The U.S. Government also is well positioned to work with other nations to gain their buy-in.
- One area of concern voiced by industry representatives is the government's attempts to mandate backdoors in encryption systems or force industry to turn over sensitive customer data. Industry believes these measures do not serve the public's long-term interest because they hamper innovation, impede the adoption of standards, erode customer confidence, and violate security best practices. Another concern raised by industry was the tendency for governments to over-regulate or push for certain certifications and accreditations that industry feels are counterproductive. Industry believes some government regulations slow the development and deployment of the latest technologies, are expensive to implement, and impede innovation. These industry representatives believe governments should focus on specifying the outcomes expected of industry, rather than engage in micro-management.

V.2 Gaps Identified by the Mobile Device Security Study Team

The results of the mobile threat assessment conducted for this report (Section IV) identified gaps in defenses in each of the threat categories as follows:

Mobile Device Technology Stack

- Delays in receiving security updates, depending on device vendor or network carrier.
- Need for continued improvements in protection of OS, TEE, baseband processor, and other device components.
- Inability of enterprises to recognize indicators of adversary activity and methods they use, e.g., zero-day vulnerabilities.
- Supply chain issues—inattention to software assurance best practices during development of mobile device components.
- Failure to use strong authentication mechanisms to critical cloud services on which the device depends.
- Much effort has gone into increasing the resilience of mobile device components against exploitation, but continued effort is required in this area that should focus not only on the mobile operating system but also on lower-level components such as TEE and baseband processors, and the software/firmware used to operate them.
- Software or firmware installed by the MNO or OEM is typically outside the purview of the mobile operating system provider, making it difficult to detect.

Mobile Applications

- Fragmented toolsets (i.e., modularization of solution sets) hinder the security and implementation of security throughout the lifecycle of mobile applications.
- Poorly defined best practices and security Systems Development Life Cycle for developers—especially for Government use.
- The lack of focus on mobile application vulnerabilities within the CVE process.
- Lack of robust information sharing of threat intelligence and integration with security tools and techniques.
- Timely notification to organizations and developers of apps affected by a vulnerability.
- Limited visibility and adoption of application vetting criteria.
- Lack of formalized standards relating security controls to data-security categorization.
- Limited knowledge of comparison between app vetting tools.
- Lack of enterprise view into the user community and mobile landscape baseline.

Mobile Networks

- Each network component of carrier infrastructure needs specific protection protocols, which appear to be rarely implemented by carriers per published reports.
- Limited or no ability to protect against geolocation of mobile devices and their users.
- The only reliable mitigation against DoS attacks on cellular towers, regions or service providers is alternate communication methods for emergencies.
- Inability to determine whether U.S. carriers have implemented GSMA Interconnect Security Monitoring Guidelines for protection against SS7 attacks.
- SS7 attack types can be used to target key U.S. Federal Government personnel both in the

United States and traveling or working overseas. U.S. carriers have established direct roaming partners that include foreign carriers based in China, Iran, Lebanon, Myanmar, Russia, Syria, Sudan, Vietnam, and Zimbabwe—all of which may actively seek to track, intercept, or attack mobile devices associated with U.S. Federal Government personnel. Government use of mobile devices overseas should be informed by threat intelligence and emerging attacker tactics, techniques, and procedures.

Device Physical Access

- There is a need for additional efforts and education to encourage users to enable screen lock on their devices regardless if a PIN, gesture, or biometric is used to protect it.
- Additional efforts are needed to defend USB-based attacks from mobile device to PC.
- Existing strong authentication solutions are not designed to complement the mobile form factor. More research is needed that incorporates the unique sensor data (motion sensor/ accelerometer, gyroscope, GPS, force sensor, capacitive sensor and camera) captured by the device to uniquely identify the registered device user.

Mobile Enterprise

- Need for improved integration of EMM/MDM solutions with mobile threat intelligence services.
- Lack of guidance on integration of EMM/MDM solutions with other enterprise security systems to enable effective response and recovery capabilities.
- Most EMMs lack the ability to directly update the mobile OS.
- More work needed to encourage enterprise adoption of capabilities, e.g., Apple's Device Enrollment Program and Samsung's Knox Mobile Enrollment.
- Immature enterprise vulnerability management processes for mobile OS and mobile apps.
- Incomplete ability of EMM solutions to identify vulnerable mobile devices.
- Incomplete ability of EMM/MDM solutions to detect sophisticated attacks against mobile devices (many jailbreak/root detection tools only detect widely known attack methods, and do little against zero-day attacks).
- Stronger mechanisms for data security and data authorization decisions need to be developed. Sensor data could be integrated into authorization decisions to provide more granular access control to selected data types based on assurance conditions.

V.3 Vulnerabilities Identified by the DHS National Coordinating Center for Communications

The mission of the DHS National Cybersecurity and Communications Integration Center (NCCIC) is to reduce the likelihood and severity of incidents that may significantly compromise the security and resilience of the nation's critical information technology and communications networks. As part of the NCCIC, the National Coordinating Center for Communications (NCC) continuously monitors national and international incidents and events that may impact national security and emergency communications. To that end, the NCC monitors SS7 and Diameter vulnerabilities and reaches these conclusions:

- DHS NCC is following published research that shows how the SS7 protocol used in all mobile phone networks is vulnerable to abuse by attackers worldwide, including eavesdropping, tracking, denial of service, and fraud.

- In addition, NCC is aware that similar SS7 vulnerabilities exist with "landline" phones and many industrial control systems.
- LTE mobile networks are using the Diameter protocol that has inherited some of the same vulnerabilities of SS7 and has been shown to be vulnerable to attack through the interworking function.
- NCC believes that all U.S. carriers are vulnerable to these exploits, resulting in risks to national security, the economy, and the Federal Government's ability to reliably execute national essential functions.
- NCC believes SS7 and Diameter vulnerabilities can be exploited by criminals, terrorists, and nation-state actors/foreign intelligence organizations.
- NCC believes many organizations appear to be sharing or selling expertise and services that could be used to spy on Americans.
- NCC is working with the FCC, the Communications Information Sharing and Analysis Center (COMM-ISAC) and other Government and non-government organizations to assess the national security and other risks associated with these vulnerabilities as well as to mitigate these risks. NCC also is aware that in response to the published research, GSMA has developed SS7 security recommendations mobile carriers can implement to partially mitigate these risks and prevent such attacks.

VI. Recommendations for Secure Mobility in Government

FISMA's security requirements apply equally to all Government programs, including the Government's mobility programs. However, as discussed throughout this report, there are unique challenges with mobility that require additional attention and these are the focus of the recommendations in this section. There are a variety of means available across the mobile ecosystem to address the threats to mobile devices and data. The following sections describe recommendations in these areas:

- Recommended Best Practices and Standards
- Need for New or Updated Policy, Standards, and Best Practices

VI.1 Best Practices and Standards Recommendations

The following survey of best practices and standards are organized by ecosystem component. Departments and Agencies should use this guidance throughout the lifecycle of their mobility programs. Adopting best practices can assist in creating a defense-in-depth posture that resists cyberattack and information compromise.

While Best Practices are recommendations, standards can be adopted to enforce a baseline security posture for specific mobile ecosystem elements. The study group recommends the Federal Government adopt a framework for mobile device security based on existing standards. Such a framework would ensure a baseline level of security for Government mobility, while providing the flexibility to address the mission needs, risk profiles, and use cases of Federal Departments and Agencies. Once standards are adopted, organizations can better manage and monitor their assets because the standardized elements have been empirically proven to operate in a repeatable secure manner that meets the requirements as defined in the standard. This takes the adopting organization to a higher level of operational maturity and thereby lessens the attack surface of the potentially vulnerable mobile ecosystem. Organizations that adopt standards and use best practices will reduce their operational burden and deliver higher quality, more secure solutions to their stakeholders and constituents.

Relevant best practices and standards for each element of the ecosystem are summarized in a table in each of the following subsections. The descriptions include a synopsis of the guidance or standard and the intended audience (e.g., CIOs, CISOs, system engineers, system architects).

In addition to the recommended guidance, this section offers recommendations for new or updated best practices and standardization for mobile ecosystem components that have satisfied the requirements under the Common Criteria Evaluation and Validation Scheme (CCEVS) to address identified gaps.

VI.1.1 Mobility Program Best Practices

Although not part of the official mobile ecosystem, Enterprise Mobility Programs address the people, processes, and technologies needed to secure an organization's data. The guiding approach is an enterprise-wide focus to allow Government agencies to apply policies and practices that fit their security posture and risk management approach. Enterprise mobility programs require governance and representation by stakeholders serving the business, information technology, cybersecurity, privacy, legal and executive functions. Table 10 lists existing guidance for enterprise mobility programs.

Table 10. Mobility Program Guidance

Document	Author	Synopsis	Audience
Mobile Computing Decision Framework (MCDF)	MTTT	The MCDF provides a holistic decision-making process that assists organizations in determining which mobile solution, if any, will support their missions.	CIOs, CISOs, system owners, senior managers, system engineers, system architects, cybersecurity professionals
Federal Mobile Computing Security Baseline	DHS, DoD, NIST	The Federal Mobile Computing Security Baseline contains the moderate baseline for the most common Federal mobility use case: Federal employees operating Agency-controlled mobile devices to access moderate impact systems on a Federal network. It includes the core controls for MDM and MAM, as well as notional controls for IAM and data management.	CIOs, CISOs, system owners, senior managers, system engineers, system architects, cybersecurity professionals
Mobile Security Reference Architecture (MSRA)	DHS, DoD, NIST	The MSRA is a flexible architecture designed to be adapted to fit the needs of any Department or Agency. Readers of the MSRA document should understand the role of each component in an architecture and the associated controls and management functions. This knowledge will enable a Department or Agency IT architect to design a "best fit" solution for their enterprise and provide a solid set of security principles and controls to secure that solution.	CIOs, CISOs, system owners, senior managers, system engineers, system architects, cybersecurity professionals
NISTIR 8144: Assessing Threats to Mobile Devices & Infrastructure Draft	NIST	This document outlines a catalogue of threats to mobile devices and associated mobile infrastructure to support development and implementation of mobile security capabilities, best practices, and security solutions to better protect enterprise IT.	CIOs, CISOs, senior managers, system engineers, system architects, cybersecurity professionals
Security Guidance for Critical Areas of Mobile Computing— Mobile Working Group	Cloud Security Alliance	This document discusses the top threats to mobile security and organizational maturity in mobile computing and provides best practice recommendations in the areas of BYOD, Mobile Authentication, App Store Security, and MDM.	CIOs, CISOs, senior managers, system engineers, system architects, cybersecurity professionals

Document	Author	Synopsis	Audience
HiMSS— Mobile Security Toolkit	Healthcare Information and Management Systems Society	This toolkit provides health care organizations resources to control and secure their mobile computing and storage devices as a part of their overall mobile security program.	CIOs, CISOs, senior managers, system engineers, system architects, cybersecurity professionals
Privacy Policy for DHS Mobile Applications, Instruction 047-01-003	DHS	This policy provides baseline privacy requirements for DHS mobile applications. Additional privacy protections may be necessary depending on the purpose and capabilities of each individual mobile application.	Privacy Officers, CIOs, CISOs, senior managers, system engineers, system architects, cybersecurity professionals

VI.1.2 Mobile Enterprise Role in the Cybersecurity Strategy and Implementation Plan (CSIP)

OMB memorandum M-16-04, the CSIP, provides overall direction for securing Federal IT environments. A key part of CSIP is the use of the CDM program. CDM is structured to determine three key characteristics of an Agency's environment:

1. What is on the Network?
2. Who is on the Network?
3. What is happening on the Network?

To obtain answers to these questions CDM establishes qualified tools and sensors for all Agency assets to allow the collection of the measures and metrics that can be used to understand the overall security posture of Federal Agencies, provide consistent reporting for FISMA, and establish risk management best practices using standard methods via the CDM Dashboard.

The isolation capabilities of mobile devices limit the ability of desktop-like layered endpoint protection techniques to monitor the state of the device, detect intrusions and respond to threats. The fact that mobile device connections to the enterprise network are sporadic and of relatively short duration renders network traffic monitoring less effective as well. Thus, it is not practical or economic to apply the methods used for the general-purpose IT environment to support the CDM objectives. Therefore, the recommendation is for the mobile space the CDM mechanisms be integrated with EMM capabilities for mobile. This step would move the CDM requirements for asset inventory, vulnerability management, configuration change management, incident detection and reporting, etc. to be within the sphere of the mobile ecosystem with an interface to the CDM structure. To support these requirements, additional FISMA metrics may need to be defined.

EMM consists of the technologies that provide MDM and MAM services for enterprise mobile application users. EMM technologies help enforce the cybersecurity posture of an organization through the centralized enforcement of device and application security configuration rules and settings. General best practices for securing enterprise use of mobile devices include the following EMM security policies:

- Restrict user and application access to hardware such as the digital camera, GPS, Bluetooth interface, USB interface, and removable storage.
- Restrict user and application access to native OS services such as the built-in web

browser, email client, calendar, contacts, application installation services, etc.

- Manage wireless network interfaces (Wi-Fi, Bluetooth, etc.)
- Automatically monitor, detect, and report when policy violations occur (such as changes from the approved security configuration baseline) and automatically take action when possible and appropriate.
- Limit or prevent access to enterprise services based on the mobile device's operating system version, vendor/brand, model, or mobile device management software client version (if applicable). This information may be unreliable.
- Enable the capability to remotely wipe a lost or stolen mobile device.

Table 11. Mobile Enterprise Best Practices Guidance

Document	Author	Synopsis	Audience
NIST SP 1800-4 Practice Guide: Mobile Device Security	NIST NCCoE	This document proposes a reference design on how to architect enterprise-class protection for mobile devices accessing corporate resources. The example solutions presented can be used by any organization implementing an EMM solution on premise or in the cloud.	Executives, cybersecurity managers, cybersecurity professionals, engineers, administrators
NIST SP 800-124r1: Guidelines for Managing the Security of Mobile Devices in the Enterprise	NIST	This publication helps organizations centrally manage the security of mobile devices. It provides recommendations for selecting, implementing, and using centralized management technologies, and explains the security concerns inherent in mobile device use and provides recommendations for securing mobile devices throughout their lifecycles.	Executives, cybersecurity managers, cybersecurity professionals, engineers, administrators
Commercial Solutions for Classified Mobile Access Capability Package	NSA	Describes a system-level framework for implementing mobile data-in-transit solutions using layered commercial products to protect classified information.	CIOs, CISOs, system owners, system engineers, system architects, cybersecurity professionals

VI.1.3 Mobile Device Technology Stack and Device Physical Access Best Practices

These best practices address multiple device types, features and components. The recommendations are sector agnostic and can be used to inform device selection and configuration for secure mobile computing.

Table 12. Device Best Practices Guidance

Document	Author	Synopsis	Audience

Document	Author	Synopsis	Audience
NIST SP 800-164 (Draft): Guidelines on Hardware-Rooted Security in Mobile Devices	NIST	This document provides a common baseline of security technologies that can be leveraged across multiple device types to provide device integrity, isolation and protected storage using hardware-based roots of trust.	OS vendors, device manufacturers, security software vendors, carriers, application software developers, cybersecurity professionals
NIST SP 800-88 Rev. 1: Guidelines for Media Sanitization	NIST	This document provides media sanitization guidelines for mobile devices based on type and intended disposition.	System owners, property managers, legal, privacy, IT professionals, cybersecurity professionals, device users
NISTIR 7981 (Draft) Mobile, PIV, and Authentication	NIST	This document analyzes various current and near-term options for remote electronic authentication from mobile devices that leverage both the investment in the PIV and PIV-I infrastructures and the unique security capabilities of mobile devices.	IT professionals, cybersecurity professionals, system architects
NIST SP 800-121 Rev1 Guide to Bluetooth Security	NIST	This publication provides information on the security capabilities of Bluetooth technologies and offers recommendations to organizations employing Bluetooth technologies for securing them effectively.	CIOs, CISOs, senior managers, system engineers, system architects, auditors, cybersecurity professionals, researchers, analysts
Mobile Device Security a Comparison of Platforms	Gartner	This assessment aids security professionals by comparing and analyzing the security controls of the most popular mobile device operating systems.	CIOs, CISOs, senior managers, system engineers, system architects, cybersecurity professionals

VI.1.4 Mobile Application Best Practices

Mobile Applications extend the basic device functionality, replicating or enhancing a Department/Agency's productivity outside of its physical locations. Mobile applications are a critical piece of the mobile ecosystem because of their access to and potential storage of mission data. These recommendations detail the need and requirements for establishing an app vetting program. Recent guidance provides sector specific recommendations for the health care and first responder communities to address their unique mobile challenges.

Table 13. Mobile Applications Best Practices Guidance

Document	Author	Synopsis	Audience

Document	Author	Synopsis	Audience
NIST SP 800-163: Vetting the Security of Mobile Applications	NIST	This document defines the app vetting process. App vetting comprises two main activities: app testing and app approval/rejection. The app testing activity involves testing an app for software vulnerabilities using services, tools, and humans to derive vulnerability reports and risk assessments. The app approval/rejection activity involves the evaluation of these reports and risk assessments along with additional criteria to determine the app's conformance with organizational security requirements and ultimately the approval or rejection of the app for deployment on the organization's mobile devices.	CIOs, CISOs, senior managers, system engineers, system architects, cybersecurity professionals, mobile application developers, mobile application testers
Adoption of Commercial Mobile Applications within the Federal Government	Digital Services Advisory Group, CIO Council	This document surveys the adoption of mobile applications in Federal Agencies and seeks to assist them in developing an approach for integrating commercial applications into their operations. Section V includes an analysis that outlines common Agency activities during the commercial mobile application lifecycle. These activities are plotted in relation to the level of organizational control versus user flexibility that can be employed to support their unique missions.	CIOs, CISOs, senior managers, system engineers, system architects, cybersecurity professionals, mobile application developers, mobile application testers
NIST SP 1800-1 Practice Guide: Securing Electronic Health Records on Mobile Devices	NIST NCCoE	NCCoE collaborated with leading health care industry groups and technology vendors to develop an example solution to show health care organizations how they can secure electronic health records on mobile devices.	CIOs, CISOs, senior managers, system engineers, system architects, cybersecurity professionals
NISTIR 8136: (Draft) Mobile Application Vetting Services for Public Safety	NIST	This document is a high-level investigation of app vetting services with the goal of enumerating the traits they exhibit that may be useful to public safety.	CIOs, CISOs, senior managers, system engineers, system architects, cybersecurity professionals, app developers, app testers

Document	Author	Synopsis	Audience
Mobile Application Single Sign-On for Public Safety and First Responders	NIST NCCoE	The vast diversity of public safety personnel, missions, and operational environments magnifies the need for a nimble authentication solution for public safety. This project will explore various multifactor authenticators currently in use or potentially offered in the future by the public safety community as their next-generation networks are brought online. The effort will not only build an interoperable solution that can accept various authenticators to speed access to online systems while maintaining an appropriate amount of security, but the project also will focus on delivering single sign-on (SSO) capabilities to both native and web-/browser-based apps.	CIOs, CISOs, System owners, senior managers, system engineers, system architects, cybersecurity professionals, app developers
Open Web Application Security Project (OWASP) - Mobile Security Project	OWASP	The OWASP Mobile Security Project is a centralized resource intended to give developers and security teams the resources necessary to build and maintain secure mobile applications. Through the project, the goal is to classify mobile security risks and provide developmental controls to reduce their impact or likelihood of exploitation.	CIOs, CISOs, system owners, senior managers, system engineers, system architects, cybersecurity professionals, app developers, app testers
Cloud Security Alliance (CSA) Mobile Application Security Testing Initiative `	Cloud Security Alliance	This initiative seeks to create a more secure cloud computing ecosystem that focuses on addressing endpoint security issues on mobile applications. It establishes secure engineering approaches to application architecture, design, testing and vetting.	CIOs, CISOs, system owners, senior managers, system engineers, system architects, cybersecurity professionals, app developers, app testers

VI.1.5 Cellular Networks Best Practices

Cellular networks are one of the primary transmission methods for voice, video, and data transport in the mobile ecosystem. Because these networks are under the control and purview of the MNO, it is imperative their architectures and technologies are understood to maintain the confidentiality, integrity, availability, and performance of enterprise operations within the mobile ecosystem.

Table 14. Cellular Networks Guidance

Document	Author	Synopsis	Audience
NISTIR 8071 (Draft) LTE Architecture Overview and Security Analysis	NIST	This document serves as a guide to the fundamentals of how LTE networks operate and explores the LTE security architecture. It also provides an analysis of the threats posed to LTE networks and supporting mitigations.	Telecommunications engineers, system administrators, cybersecurity professionals, security researchers
SS7 Interconnect Security Monitoring Guidelines (GSMA FS.11)	GSMA	This document serves as a guide for MNOs on current mitigations for SS7/Diameter threats specifically related to interconnection fraud.	Telecommunications engineers, system administrators, cybersecurity professionals, security researchers

Recommendation: When procuring mobile devices and related services, all Government organizations should include requirements that carriers mitigate SS7/Diameter exploits and other monitoring, tracking, invasion of privacy, and denial of service vulnerabilities.

VI.1.6 Best Practices Summary

All the guidance documents described in sections VI.1.1 through VI.1.5 provide an element of security to the complex mobile ecosystem. Any one piece of guidance alone will not secure an enterprise. To thwart today's advanced attackers, all elements of the mobile ecosystem must be addressed. From device selection, to app vetting, mobile device and application deployment and management, to secure architectures/communications and connections to on-premise legacy data stores and cloud technologies, each component of the ecosystem is critical to ensuring the secure and reliable delivery of mission data. Neglect of any one component would inject vulnerability into the ecosystem and potentially jeopardize the diverse missions of the U.S. Government.

VI.1.7 Recommended Standards

The Common Criteria is an international standard by which technology types are independently certified to operate to requirements as specified in the Protection Profiles for each technology type. The independent evaluation ensures the purchaser of a technology that it is designed and built to meet a high and consistent level of security assurance. Additionally, it reduces duplication of effort required for security testing and validation. In the United States, the NIAP is responsible for the U.S. implementation of the program. While not currently mandated for use in Federal Departments and Agencies, it could be used to speed secure adoption of mobile ecosystem components that have defined Protection Profiles.

There are also mobile standards bodies leveraged by commercial industry. Organizations such as GlobalPlatform and the Trusted Computing Group specialize in promulgating standards in their respective specialty areas. Ensuring selected mobile ecosystem vendors comply with these standards will result in greater interoperability and reduced risk to the mobile ecosystem.

Table 15. Standards Recommendations

Document	Author	Synopsis	Audience
Mobile Applications			
NIAP Protection Profile for Application Software	NIAP	This assurance standard specifies information security functionality requirements for application software, including mobile applications. This standard specifies requirements to ensure that applications correctly implement security functionality and conform to norms of application behavior.	CIOs, CISOs, senior managers, system engineers, system architects, cybersecurity professionals
Mobile Device Technology Stack and Device Physical Access			
NIAP Protection Profile for Mobile Device Fundamentals 3.0	NIAP	This assurance standard specifies information security requirements for mobile devices for use in an enterprise. A mobile device in the context of this assurance standard is a device that is composed of a hardware platform and its system software. The mobile device provides essential services such as cryptographic services, data-at-rest protection, and key storage services to support the secure operation of applications on the device. Additional security features such as security policy enforcement, application mandatory access control, anti-exploitation features, user authentication, and software integrity protection are implemented to address threats.	CIOs, CISOs, senior managers, system engineers, system architects, cybersecurity professionals
Global Platform Specification for Trusted Execution Environment/ Global Platform Specification for Secure Element Management	GlobalPlatform	GlobalPlatform identifies, develops and publishes technical specifications and market configurations that facilitate the secure and interoperable deployment and management of multiple-embedded applications on secure chip technology. Its proven technology is regarded as the international industry standard for building a trusted end-to-end solution that serves multiple users and supports several business models.	Product vendors, OEM manufacturers, testers
Trusted Computing Group Specifications for Trusted Platform Module	Trusted Computing Group	Trusted Platform Module (TPM) is an international standard for a secure cryptoprocessor, which is a dedicated microprocessor designed to secure hardware by integrating cryptographic keys into devices.	OEM manufacturers, mobile network operators, mobile service providers

Document	Author	Synopsis	Audience
Mobile Enterprise			
NIAP Protection Profile for Mobile Device Management Version 2.0	NIAP	MDM products allow enterprises to apply security policies to mobile devices such as smartphones and tablets. The purpose of these policies is to establish a security posture adequate to permit mobile devices to process enterprise data and connect to enterprise network resources. This protection profile specifies baseline requirements for MDM systems.	CIOs, CISOs, senior managers, system engineers, system architects, cybersecurity professionals
NIAP Protection Profile - Extended Package for Mobile Device Management Agents 2.0	NIAP	This extended package describes baseline security requirements for MDM agents. An MDM agent is the mobile device-resident component of an MDM product.	CIOs, CISOs, senior managers, system engineers, system architects, cybersecurity professionals

Departments/Agencies should leverage NIAP Protection Profiles or equivalent security criteria for baseline requirements in mobile computing products used in the Federal Government.

Existing policy requires that information assurance (IA) and IA-enabled IT products used in the NSS be evaluated against NIAP-approved PPs. This includes all mobile devices, mobile operating systems, enterprise mobility management products, and many mobile applications used to process classified and sensitive unclassified information for the DoD and Intelligence Community. As of September 2016, all major mobile device vendors provide PP-certified products that are on NIAP's PCL.

- NIAP or other security criteria could be used in the following ways: Mobile applications that provide IA services—such as email clients, web browsers, VoIP clients, and VPN Clients—should be evaluated and selected from the NIAP PCL. Applications that do not provide such services should be vetted against the requirements found in the Requirements for Vetting Mobile Apps[165] from the Application Software PP so Departments/Agencies have information on which to base risk decisions. DHS should continue its work with NIAP to automate testing of mobile apps against the PP's app vetting requirements.
- The Federal Government should select mobile devices that have been evaluated to meet a minimum level of security, e.g., from the NIAP PCL and the PP for Mobile Device Fundamentals or other Government approved product lists.
- Enterprise mobility management products purchased by the Federal Government should be selected from the NIAP PCL or other approved product lists. Products on the NIAP PCL have been evaluated against the PP for Mobile Device Management or the Extended Package for Mobile Device Management Agents.
- As additional mobility-focused PPs are developed, products of the technologies

---

[165] https://www.niap-ccevs.org/pp/pp_app_v1.2_table-reqs.htm

addressed by the new PPs purchased by the Federal Government should be selected from the NIAP PCL and evaluated against the new PPs.

VI.2 New or Updated Policy, Standards, and Best Practices

VI.2.1 New or Updated Best Practices

There are several areas of guidance that could be updated and or improved to facilitate a higher level of assurance for Government operations within the mobile ecosystem. Analyzing the subset of guidance listed in Section VI.1, most of the guidance was produced between 2010-2013, which was during the advent of the adoption of mobility within the Federal Government. This guidance, though still applicable, should be updated based on lessons learned, new threat information, and new technologies that were unavailable or not mature enough to recommend adoption during that period. The mobile landscape changes more quickly than the traditional PC- and server-based refresh cycle. Major operating system releases, connected accessories and new device functions are developed and released in a continuous cycle. Therefore, the best practice guidance also should be kept up to date on an ongoing or more frequent basis.

Mobile Applications. There is a need to create security guidelines for mobile application development. This is the corollary activity to the successful execution of a Department/ Agency's app vetting program. The tools market in this space has matured greatly since the app vetting guidance was created in 2015, however, developer-focused guidance that communicates best practices on how to securely code, package and release applications is still lacking. Organizations such as OWASP and mobile OS vendors provide some content in this area. However, these practices have not been collected and/or abstracted into a unified guide for the development community. This represents a gap in the pipeline necessary to secure the mobile applications against threats targeting Government or personal data stored on these devices, either of which could seriously undermine the secure and reliable delivery of services by the U.S. Government.

Signaling System 7/Diameter. SS7/Diameter vulnerabilities are a specific area of concern for the Federal Government. SS7 and Diameter protocol vulnerabilities cannot be completely "fixed," but the risks to networks and subscribers can be mitigated greatly if effective action is taken. U.S. carriers can take additional measures to safeguard the privacy of their subscribers and protect their networks from intrusion, but it is difficult to obtain objective evidence of carrier compliance with best practices, because of the lack of legal authority. Further investigation is required to fully answer this question. However, DHS recommends Government organizations that provide mobile information services contract with commercial service providers to conduct independent third-party SS7/Diameter and other security penetration testing, to baseline vulnerabilities and develop risk mitigations.

Results from penetration testing conducted with a U.S. carrier/operator through January 2016 have shown network exposure to these flaws that allow tracking of any mobile phone, eavesdropping on conversations, and unauthorized entities to change user profiles and information on the network. Carriers should take the necessary steps to prevent mobile network abuse scenarios via multiple techniques. Such techniques include baselining network traffic, use of IDSs, vulnerability assessments, penetration testing, and advanced call delivery troubleshooting. Results of such testing should be shared with the COMM-ISAC. Varying approaches by operators/carriers to test their network may identify multiple attack vectors. The community must work together to address and mitigate these vulnerabilities.

A carrier's ability to limit their network's exposure to SS7/Diameter exploits and guard against monitoring, tracking, invasion of privacy and denial of service should be considered by all Government organizations when procuring mobile devices and related services. Different levels of protection should be developed and included as standard contractual service agreements related to network and device security, similar to those developed for computer security.

Several commercial products exist that offer varying levels of security for both SS7 and Diameter. Diameter is a more recent iteration of signaling protocol that was designed with security in mind, establishing the use of IPsec/TLS and certificate-based authentication. However, SS7 is expected to be in use for at least 20 years more. Diameter is currently used by a limited number of operators for LTE roaming and signaling transport. 3GPP standards require use of the Diameter interface for signaling transport in the LTE Evolved Packet Core (EPC). A lot of the SS7 design has been ported to Diameter and there is evidence of some of the same security issues found in SS7 have been carried over (e.g., there is still no end-to-end authentication for subscribers). Vulnerability assessment should include testing SS7 exploits against Diameter-supported network devices that bridge into 2G/3G networks.

The NCC has held many meetings with its federal and industry partners to alert them about SS7 and threats posed by rogue base stations. Additionally, NCC has been working with industry and our Federal partners to assess the overall risks and mitigation options. For example, the NCC has:

- Discussed SS7-related issues with AT&T, T-Mobile, Sprint, Verizon, and other members of the COMM-ISAC to better understand the problem and to hear the carriers' perspective on how best to mitigate SS7 related risks.
- Requested from a carrier the results of their SS7 penetration testing.
- Participates as a member of the newly formed Communications Security, Reliability, and Interoperability Council (CSRIC) V Working Group #10 related to SS7 and Diameter vulnerabilities.

Several mobile security vendors offer SS7 threat detection and vulnerability mitigation capabilities. The steps DHS anticipates the carriers will need to undertake to effectively mitigate these vulnerabilities are as follows:

- **Perform Vulnerability Assessment.** Carriers should contract with an independent security vendor to identify vulnerabilities in their networks and assess their level of security. Each carrier can agree to have noninvasive penetration testing performed on its network or have the security vendor assess vulnerabilities based on traffic traces provided by the carrier.
- **Implement a Monitoring System**. Carriers should set up a SS7/Diameter-specific firewall and IDS. There is no way to stop unauthorized SS7 Message Signal Units (MSUs) from being injected into networks. Therefore, a solution must be implemented to recognize and mitigate them before they can reach their intended destination. This could be done by placing firewalls at network interconnects, for example Signaling Transfer Points (STP) and International Gateway Exchanges, and auditing MSUs as they pass through. The monitoring system will alert the carrier of suspicious activity/events based on a vulnerability knowledge database. The firewall/IDSs will need to be augmented by

the knowledge obtained from independent SS7/Diameter penetration tests/vulnerability assessments.

- **Perform Continuous Assessment and Protection.** SS7-specific Intrusion Protection System (IPS) packets flowing through firewalls would be decoded and inspected to determine where configured rules can be applied and traffic flow filtered accordingly. Filtering rules could be applied at multiple levels of the SS7 stack. For example, rules could be applied as blacklists for MSUs to block, whitelists that block all MSUs of a certain type except those specified and greylists for events to log. Mobile phone operating systems could be modified to alert end-users of greylisted MSUs that are attempting to use resources on their mobile phone so the users can determine if the MSUs are acceptable. MSU filtering could be applied at multiple layers of the SS7 stack and use data/intelligence from operators as well as statistics gathered by observing previous traffic to ensure maximum optimization. A firewall properly configured using these tools could block unauthorized MSUs without blocking legitimate ones and harming valued services. This can be done by either the carrier or security vendor. For Government users, the Government should be involved in decisions on when or how to block unauthorized location tracking and interception of voice and data traffic.

VI.2.2 New or Updated Standards

Standards to Address Carrier Network Vulnerabilities. While many standards are open and available for review, others are restricted to members of the standards group, making it difficult for the Government to assess the relevant security portions of the standards. The GSMA Roaming and Interconnect Fraud and Security (RIFS) Subgroup is engaged currently in developing standards for SS7 filtering, SS7 monitoring, Diameter security, roaming guidelines and firewall rules for Mobile Application Part (MAP) v2/3. Those documents are GSMA-confidential and accessible only to members.

Government Participation in Standards Development Organizations. Numerous American industry representatives raised concerns with the study group that the U.S. Government was not represented on relevant standards bodies. These representatives feel that this puts the U.S. information and communications technology sector at a competitive disadvantage globally.

FirstNet has the legislative responsibility to represent the Nationwide Public Safety Broadband Network (NPSBN) in international standards bodies. Since its creation in 2012, FirstNet has and continues to aggressively represent the interests of public safety and future NPSBN users at international standards bodies such as 3GPP.

Recommendation: DHS and other relevant federal agencies should review and make recommendations on GSMA and other mobile device/network security related standards bodies. Best practice recommendations should be established for Government and critical infrastructure stakeholders to help protect the integrity, confidentiality, and availability of mobile devices and networks that support essential functions.

VI.2.3 New or Updated Policy

Mobility Program and FISMA. DHS recommends OMB develop new guidance specific to the mobile ecosystem and metrics for measuring Department/Agency performance in implementing the guidance.

Vulnerability Management. Many of the existing mechanisms that support security function visibility, such as those that are part of the National Vulnerability Database (NVD) managed by US-CERT, need modification and updating to reconcile the difference in attributes between the current general purpose IT infrastructure and what is required for mobile computing. This work would include changes to CVE/Common Weakness Enumeration (CWE) and Common Platform Enumeration (CPE).

Cellular Networks. Request carriers voluntarily provide DHS SS7 vulnerability assessment or penetration testing results to establish risk baseline.

International Travel. The study group recommends that Federal Departments and Agencies develop or enhance, where needed, policies and procedures covering Government use of mobile devices overseas based on threat intelligence and emerging attacker tactics, techniques, and procedures.

VII.   Gaps in DHS Authorities

Over the last two years, U.S. carriers have acknowledged to the NCC that SS7 and Diameter vulnerabilities potentially exist in their networks, but they have not quantified or characterized the extent or nature of these risks to their network.

Likewise, they have not quantified to the Government what they are doing to mitigate risks to Government, commercial, and private users. DHS is particularly concerned that many foreign vendors appear to be sharing or selling expertise and services that can be used to spy on Americans.

New laws and authorities may be needed to enable the Government to independently assess the national security and other risks associated with SS7- and Diameter-dependent networks. Likewise, new laws or authorities[166] may be needed for the Government to monitor SS7- and Diameter-based attacks and exploitations in near real-time.

Existing DHS NCC authorities include:

- The President has charged the Secretary of DHS to assess continuity communications (including mobile communications).
- Also, under Executive Order 13618, the Secretary of DHS has responsibilities to assure resilient communications infrastructure.[167]

There are gaps in DHS legal authorities to test, verify, or assess and mitigate risks relating to the security of mobile devices within the Federal Government:

- Gap 1: DHS has no legal authority to require mobile carriers to assess risks relating to the

---

[166] Federal agencies such as the FCC and FTC may have authorities over some of these issues.
[167] Assignment of National Security and Emergency Preparedness Communications Functions, July 6, 2012

security of mobile network infrastructure as it impacts the Government's use of mobile devices.

- Gap 2: While DHS has the authority to evaluate voluntarily provided mobile carrier network information, DHS has no legal authority to compel mobile carrier network owners/operators to provide information to assess the security of these critical communications networks.

VIII. Next Steps

The results of this study show the need to address challenges that threaten the use of mobile devices by the U.S. Government and the entirety of the mobile ecosystem.

To address these areas of concern, DHS proposes the following:

- FISMA metrics should be enhanced to focus on securing mobile devices through the Federal CIO Council's MTTT. Metrics for consideration include mobile operating systems, mobile device authentication methods, and volume of mobile device user traffic not going through the Department's/Agency's Trusted Internet Connection (TIC).
- The DHS CDM program should address the security of mobile devices and applications with capabilities to be at parity with other network devices (e.g., workstations and servers), and NPPD's definition of critical infrastructure should include mobile network infrastructure.
- DHS S&T HSARPA Cyber Security Division should continue its work in Mobile Application Security to ensure the secure use of mobile applications for Government use.

Potential areas for additional research or partnerships within DHS include:

- Creating a new applied R&D program in securing mobile network infrastructure to address current and emerging challenges impeding mobile technology.
- Establishing a new program for applied research to operations in advanced defensive security tools and methods for addressing mobile malware and vulnerabilities, including new ways to handle CVE generation for mobile and mobile threat information sharing, e.g., Structured Threat Information eXpression (STIX™), and Trusted Automated eXchange of Indicator Information (TAXII™). DHS should coordinate this initiative with existing efforts within DoD.
- Coordinating the adoption and advancement of mobile security technologies recommended in this report into operational programs such as Einstein and CDM to ensure future capabilities include protection and defense against mobile threats.
- Developing cooperative arrangements and capabilities with commercial mobile network operators to detect, protect and respond to threats (e.g., rogue IMSI catchers and SS7/Diameter vulnerabilities) that impede the confidentiality, integrity and availability of Government communications; and if necessary, extend the legal authorities of NPPD to achieve these objectives.

Additional topics that require a response by the Federal Government are:

- The U.S. Government should continue[168] and enhance its active participation in international standards bodies so it can represent America's national interest with the private sector in the development of consensus-based voluntary mobile security standards and best practices.
- Continued development of the NIST draft *Mobile Threat Catalogue* with additional

---

[168] FirstNet has the legislative responsibility to represent the NPSBN in international standards bodies. Since its creation in 2012, FirstNet has and continues to aggressively represent the interests of public safety and future NPSBN users at international standards bodies such as 3GPP.

cooperation from industry and the inclusion of emerging threats and defenses and additional risk metrics for mobile threats.

- Federal Departments and Agencies should, where needed, develop or enhance policies and procedures regarding Government use of mobile devices overseas based on threat intelligence and emerging attacker tactics, techniques, and procedures.

IX.   Appendices

Appendix A: Request for Information: Mobile Security Threats and Defenses

RFI and survey form were posted on FedBizOpps at:
https://www.fbo.gov/index?s=opportunity&mode=form&tab=core&id=bc457545615649b4371c
edd9de371bb9

Solicitation Number: QTA00NS16SDI0003   **Notice Type**: Special Notice
Added: Jul 07, 2016 2:34 pm

Synopsis:

This RFI is intended to afford the mobile and cellular/Wi-Fi industry and mobile security researchers the opportunity to identify their technical capabilities (current and/or future) to address risks posed by the Federal Government's use of mobile technologies as described in Section II of this RFI and any standards that should be developed or adapted to support enterprise mobile security implementation (including networks and services supporting emergency communications, priority services, alerting, etc.) from the Government's perspective. The Government is soliciting input on products, services, capabilities and technologies that address threats related to the Government's use of mobile devices and services. Responses will be used for the congressionally required study and will help the Government understand the range of products and technologies available to protect the mobile ecosystem. It will also help the Government to identify gaps-areas that provide opportunities for industry, Government and academic researchers to collaborate on advancing technologies and/or standards. We also are requesting respondents to identify considerations, constraints and recommendations (including industry standards and best practices) the Government should consider for its assessment of threats and available mitigations.

This RFI is issued solely for market research, information and planning purposes and is not to be construed as a commitment by the Government. This RFI does not in any way imply a planned or pending procurement action by the United States Government. No solicitation exists; therefore, do not request a copy of a solicitation. Responses to this RFI will not constitute an offer and shall not be accepted as the basis for forming a binding contract. The Government is not seeking proposals at this time and will not accept unsolicited proposals in response to this RFI. The Government will not reimburse any respondent for any costs associated with information submitted in response to this RFI.

Appendix B: List of Responding Organizations

- 4K Solutions, LLC
- Absolute Software
- AdaptiveMobile Security Ltd.
- Advanced Cyber Security
- AirWatch (VMWare)
- Akamai
- Applied Communication Sciences
- Appthority
- AT&T
- Better Mobile Security
- Blackberry
- BlueRISC
- Cellbusters
- Check Point
- Cisco Systems
- CTIA
- Cyber adAPT
- Dexter Edward, LLC
- Duo Security
- Gadget Guard
- Galois
- Google, Inc.
- HRL Laboratories

- IBM
- Intel Security
- Intelligent Automation, Inc.
- IPTA & Akamai
- Kaprica Security Inc.
- Kryptowire
- Lookout
- MobileIron
- Optio Labs
- Oracle
- Procera Networks
- Qualcomm Technologies
- Rivetz
- RML Business Consulting
- RunSafe Security Inc.
- Samsung
- SecureLogix
- Squadra Technologies
- Temple University & Sentar, Inc.
- Trustonic
- TSI
- Verizon
- Waverly Labs

Appendix C: Government-Industry One-on-One Interview Questions

1. Have you had a chance to read the RFI and does your organization plan to respond?

2. Does your product's functionality fit neatly within one or more of the five threat types discussed in the RFI? If not, is that because you disagree with the categories or because you think there is a significant missing category?

3. What industry, or type of business, would you benchmark yourself against?

4. What are your major objectives as they relate to mobile security?

5. Do you view security, specifically mobile security, as a significant market force? Would you contrast that with privacy?

6. What are your top three existing mobile threats? Top five?

6a. What are the top three mobile threats that you feel have been completely or partially mitigated by a solution provided by you or another vendor?

7. Are there aspects of the total mobile ecosystem that you believe perform well as it relates to security of the overall system or some subsection?

8. Are there segments of the total mobile ecosystem that you feel or know to be insecure which are outside either the capabilities or the influence of your organization?

9. Do you view the U.S. Federal Government as a primary customer?

9a. What impediments do you encounter to having the U.S. Federal Government as a customer?

10. Which branch, department, or agency of the Federal Government most effects your approach to mobile security?

11. Based on your previous experience of rolling out new technologies, how is your organization positioned to handle new, or modified, technology requirements from the Federal Government?

12. Has your organization participated in the Federal Government's National Information Assurance Partnership (NIAP), either through seeking Common Criteria security evaluation of your products and/or through participation in NIAP's Mobility Technical Community, which seeks to develop future security requirements for mobility products in a collaborative environment?

12a. Do you have any feedback you wish to share or suggestions for how the Federal Government can best evaluate the security of mobility products to be used in sensitive environments, including any specific issues with current approaches?

12b. If not already participating, would you be willing to participate in working groups with the Federal Government and industry to establish security requirements or best practices for mobility products?

13.   Is your organization a member of any standards bodies or professional organizations such as 3GPP, the GSMA, or CTIA?

13a. If so, do you feel they adequately represent your organization's best interests?

13b. If not, do you feel they obstruct your product(s) or create an unfair market?

13c. Do you feel that those organizations or any others work to create an overall secure mobile ecosystem? If not, do you believe they work against securing the overall mobile ecosystem because of profit motivations or simply a lack of understanding or a lack of regulation?

14.   Does your organization make use of, follow, or publish any best practices guidelines for any part of the mobile ecosystem? If so, does this include any security best practices?

15.   Today's mobile operating systems protect against malicious behaviors in part by implementing sandboxing mechanisms that strictly control interactions between applications and the underlying device. However, these mechanisms have the side effect of limiting the capabilities of third-party security products that on our traditional desktop computers would typically run at a highly privileged level where they can observe system behavior for anomalies.

What do you see as the role of third-party security products compared to the role of security features inherently provided by the mobile device and by the mobile device vendor or mobile operating system vendor's surrounding ecosystem (e.g., screening of app store submissions) in assuring the security of enterprise mobile devices used in highly sensitive environments?

15a. For enterprise mobile devices used in highly sensitive environments, we are concerned about targeted attacks from sophisticated attackers, including methods such as the use of previously unseen exploits ("zero-days") and efforts to evade app store security screening or other detection mechanisms. Do you have any data on the prevalence of these types of attacks? Do you believe that existing security approaches are sufficient for these environments? Are there additional recommendations, beyond what might be recommended for typical consumer use, that you would make for use of mobile devices in these environments?

15b. Do you have a method or plan for broader distribution of threat and vulnerability information with/through entities such as US-CERT? If not, how would you recommend the Government obtain such information on a timely basis and share it with Government agencies and the public?

16. Various parts of the mobile ecosystem are regulated and overseen by the FCC, the FTC, the Department of Commerce, the State Department, DHS, and the Department of Justice. Do you feel that having so many agencies directly contributes or contributes in any way to security problems and threats?

17. Have any new regulations, or policies, required that you make significant changes to your product design or systems architecture?

17a. Are there any specific objectives, or "pain-points," that you would like to see specifically addressed by regulations?

17b. Do you feel the current regulatory structure provides a level playing field across the mobile ecosystem or does it favor specific sectors?

18. Are there laws and regulations currently on the books in the United States that you believe create security problems for parts of the mobile ecosystem? Are you aware of any proposed laws and regulations that you believe will create security problems for parts of the mobile ecosystem?

19. Does the global nature of the total mobile ecosystem concern you? In other words, does the fact that laws and regulations of other countries impact the design and architecture of aspects of the mobile ecosystem undermine security and specifically security as it relates to the U.S. Federal Government?

20. How do you feel DHS can best work to increase the overall security of the mobile ecosystem?

21. Are there any specific objectives, or "pain-points" that you would like to see addressed within the Mobile Security Study?

22. If there was one underlying theme or a single thesis of the mobile security study what would you like it to be?

Other Comments or Remarks

Appendix D: Organizations Interviewed

- Apple

- AT&T

- CTIA

- Cyber adAPT

- Google, Inc.

- Kryptowire

- Lookout, Inc.

- Microsoft

- MobileIron

- ProofPoint

- Qualcomm Technologies, Inc.

- Samsung Electronics America, Inc.

- VMWare AirWatch

Appendix E: Adversarial Tactics, Techniques, and Common Knowledge

The MITRE Corporation built the Adversarial Tactics, Techniques, and Common Knowledge (ATT&CK™) model and framework[169] to describe the actions an attacker may take while operating within an enterprise network after a successful exploit. It expands the post-exploitation stages of the Cyber Attack Lifecycle into 10 tactic categories, each consisting of specific publicly observed techniques that attackers have used against Windows enterprise PCs. The 10 tactic categories, as adapted for the mobile environment, are described in the paragraphs that follow.

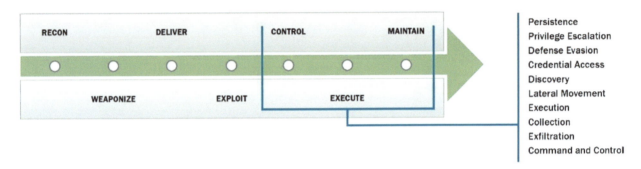

Figure 18: Stages of the Cyber Attack Lifecycle with the ATT&CK™ Tactic Categories

- **Persistence.** Any access, action, or configuration change to a mobile device that gives an attacker a persistent presence on the device. Attackers often will need to maintain access to mobile devices through interruptions such as device resets.
- **Privilege Escalation.** Techniques that allow an attacker to obtain a higher level of permissions on the mobile device. Attackers may enter the mobile device with very limited privileges and may be required to take advantage of a device weakness to obtain higher privileges necessary to successfully carry out their mission objectives.
- **Defense Evasion.** Techniques an attacker may use to evade detection or avoid other defenses. These actions may be the same as or variations of techniques in other categories with the added benefit of subverting a defense or mitigation. Defense evasion may be considered a set of attributes the attacker applies to all other phases of the operation.
- **Credential Access.** Techniques resulting in access to credentials that enable an attacker to assume an identity and access other systems.
- **Discovery.** Techniques that enable an attacker to gain knowledge about the characteristics of the mobile device or other systems.
- **Lateral Movement.** Techniques that enable an attacker to access or control other systems.
- **Collection or Execution.** Techniques used to identify and gather information from the

---

[169] © 2016 The MITRE Corporation. ATT&CK and the ATT&CK Matrix are trademarks of The MITRE Corporation. https://attack.mitre.org/

mobile device prior to exfiltration. For the mobile adaptation of ATT&CK™, execution more broadly refers to techniques used by attackers to perform their mission objectives.

- **Exfiltration.** Techniques and attributes that result or aid in the attacker removing files and information from the targeted mobile device.
- **Command and Control.** Techniques used by the attacker to communicate with mobile devices under their control.

Many use cases exist for the ATT&CK™ framework. Most notably for this study, it provides a means to:

1. Concisely represent techniques used by an attacker in a matrix format that depicts tactics and techniques across the mobile ecosystem—before and after threat exploit.
2. Use that matrix to demonstrate the threat events of a specific attacker campaign.
3. Perform gap analyses of current defensive techniques.

The ATT&CK™ model was originally built for enterprise PCs. MITRE, as part of its work on NCCoE's draft *Mobile Threat Catalogue*, adapted ATT&CK for the mobile environment, defining the techniques an attacker would use in each tactic category in that environment. In addition to modeling post-exploitation tactics and techniques, it is also important to be able to model the pre-exploitation tactics and techniques that are used by attackers to gain an initial presence on a mobile device. The following pre-exploitation tactic categories were defined:

- **Malicious App Delivery via Official App Store.** Malicious applications are a common attack vector used by attackers to gain a presence on mobile devices. Mobile devices often are configured to allow application installation only from the official app store (e.g., Google Play Store or Apple App Store). This category refers to tactics and techniques that can be used to place a malicious application in an official app store that enable the application to be installed on targeted devices.
- **Malicious App Delivery via Other Means.** This category refers to tactics and techniques that can be used to install a malicious application on targeted mobile devices without involving one of the official app stores. Even if it is possible for an attacker to place a malicious application in an official app store, they may choose not to do so due to increased potential risk of detection or other reasons.
- **Exploit via Cellular Network.** This category refers to tactics and techniques executed via the cellular network to gain control of targeted mobile devices.
- **Exploit via Internet.** This category refers to tactics and techniques involving the mobile device's connectivity to the Internet that could be used by an attacker to gain control of targeted mobile devices.
- **Exploit via Physical Access.:** This category refers to tactics and techniques involving physical access to the device that could be used by an attacker to gain control of the device.
- **Supply Chain.** This category refers to tactics and techniques involving supply chain access that could be used by an attacker to gain control of targeted mobile devices.
- **Exploit via Compromised Enterprise Management.** This category refers to tactics and techniques that allow an attacker to leverage control of an EMM system to gain control of targeted mobile devices.

The figures below demonstrate the use of the mobile device ATT&CK™ matrices to portray the tactics and techniques used in the recent Pegasus spyware threat against iOS devices, based on the technical analysis of Pegasus published by Lookout.[170] As described in Section IV.2, Pegasus is an example of highly advanced surveillance-ware allegedly used in an attempted exploitation of an iOS device belonging to Ahmed Mansoor, "an internationally recognized human rights defender based in the UAE."

As described in Lookout's report and in Citizen Lab's analysis,[171] SMS messages were sent to Mansoor's iPhone containing webpage links. Rather than opening the links, Mansoor sent copies of the messages to Citizen Lab. Citizen Lab and Lookout determined that clicking on the links led to webpages containing malicious code designed to exploit vulnerabilities in the mobile device's web browser and in the underlying operating system to install spyware on the device.

Figure 19 is an ATT&CK matrix depicting pre-exploitation tactics and techniques, with the methods used by the attacker in the Pegasus attack (as described in Lookout's report) highlighted in red.

Malicious App Delivery via Official App Store	Malicious App Delivery via Other Means	Exploit via Cellular Network	Exploit via Internet	Exploit via Physical Access	Supply Chain	Exploit via Compromised Enterprise Mgmt
App analysis environment detection and evasion	Email attachment	Malicious SMS/MMS content	Malicious iOS Config Profile		Malicious compiler or other SW dev tools	Steal EMM administrator credentials
	Web site link	SMS link to malicious web content	Malicious web content	Malicious charging station		
Fake developer accounts	SMS link	Malicious update from carrier	Malicious media file	From compromised PC	Malicious or exploitable 3rd party SW libraries	Push malicious app via EMM
Stolen developer credentials	Stolen enterprise signing key	Exploit baseband radio vulnerability		Exploit unlocked or vulnerable bootloader		
Remotely install app				PIN/Password Guessing or Brute Force		Reset/remove device screen lock
Repackage or impersonate legit app				Biometric Spoofing		

Based on Lookout's Technical Analysis of Pegasus Spyware

Figure 19: Matrix Depicting Pegasus iOS Spyware Pre-Exploitation Techniques

---

[170] https://info.lookout.com/rs/051-ESQ-475/images/lookout-pegasus-technical-analysis.pdf
[171] https://citizenlab.org/2016/08/million-dollar-dissident-iphone-zero-day-nso-group-uae/

Figure 20 depicts the post-exploit tactics and techniques adapted for the mobile environment; tactics appear in the top row and example techniques are in the columns. For example, the Privilege Escalation tactic category includes techniques explained in Section IV.2—exploitation of vulnerabilities in the mobile OS, the Trusted Execution Environment, or in the mobile device's firmware. The techniques listed under the Collection/Execution category—access sensitive data, track user location, lock or wipe device, activate camera or microphone to record user—were described in multiple threat categories. Again, the Pegasus attack is used as an example, with the observed tactics and techniques reported by Lookout highlighted in red.

Persistence	Privilege Escalation	Defense Evasion	Credential Access	Discovery	Lateral Movement	Collection/Execution	Exfiltration/Cmd and Ctrl
Modify OS Kernel / Boot Partition	Exploit OS Vulnerability	Obfuscated or Encrypted Code	Credentials in Files	Application Enumeration	Exploit Cloud Services (e.g. Google Play remote app install)	Access Sensitive Data	Commonly Used Port
	Exploit TEE Vulnerability	Dynamic Code Execution	Network Sniffing	Device Type Enumeration		Lock User out of Device	Data Encrypted
Modify System Partition	Exploit Baseband Vulnerability	Disguise Root/Jailbreak Indicators	User Interface Spoofing	File and Directory Discovery	Attack PC via USB	Wipe Device Data	Multiband Communication
Modify TEE			Capture Codes sent via SMS	Local Network Configuration Discovery	Exploit enterprise servers/PCs over network	Microphone/Camera Recordings	Alternate Network Mediums (e.g. SMS, NFC, Bluetooth)
App Auto-start at Device Boot		Abuse Accessibility Features	Credentials in Device Logs	Local Network Connections Discovery		Location Tracking	
Use Android Device Admin Access to Prevent Removal			Capture Clipboard Data	Operating System Discovery		Screen and Keypress Capture	Standard App Layer Protocol
			Android Intent or iOS URL Scheme Hijacking	Process Discovery		Premium SMS Fraud	
Modify Android Cached Executable Code			Malicious Keyboard App	Security Software Discovery		Network Traffic Redirection	
						Access Contact List, Call Log, or Calendar	

Based on Lookout's Technical Analysis of Pegasus Spyware

Figure 20: Matrix Depicting Pegasus iOS Spyware Post-Exploitation Techniques

Using Other Elements of the Mobile Ecosystem to Access Voice or Data

In many cases, an attacker may not need access to the mobile device itself to perform his or her objectives. For example, Section IV.4 describes threats posed by an attacker with access to the network infrastructure such as eavesdropping on or manipulating communication to or from the mobile device, denial of service, installing a rogue base station or Wi-Fi access point, or exploiting SS7 vulnerabilities. Since these methods are not carried out on or through the device, a different set of tactics and techniques was defined. The tactic categories shown in the matrix below align to the mobile security threat categories: networks, mobile device technology stack, mobile enterprise, and physical access. The example techniques under each tactic category were described in the relevant sections (e.g., general and cellular network tactics and techniques were explained in Section IV.4).

General Network Based	Cellular Network Based	Device Vendor Cloud-Based	Enterprise Management Based	Physical Based
Eavesdrop on Device Comms (Voice or Data)	Downgrade to insecure protocols	Remotely track device without authorization		Obtain device backups containing sensitive data
		Remotely wipe device without authorization		Crypto side-channel attack to steal keys and decrypt data
Jamming or Denial of Service		Obtain device backups containing sensitive data	Obtain audit logs or other sensitive data	Physical eavesdropping on device use
Rogue Access Points or Base Stations (e.g. to eavesdrop or modify data or track device location)				
Modify Network Packets	Exploit SS7 to redirect calls/SMS			
Man-in-the-Middle Attacks				
	Exploit SS7 to track device location			

Figure 21: Matrix Depicting Attacker Tactics and Techniques without Device Access

Assessing State of Defenses Against Mobile Threats

A frequent use of the ATT&CK™ Matrix model is to depict the current state of defensive techniques and illustrate where gaps exist. The following figures provided color-coded depictions of the state of available mitigation or detection techniques for the mobile tactics and techniques. The red boxes indicate techniques for which there is no ability or minimal ability to mitigate or detect use of the technique. The yellow boxes indicate techniques for which there is a partial ability to mitigate or detect use of the technique. The green boxes indicate techniques for which there is a full ability to mitigate or detect use of the technique. The colors were chosen based on the analysis of the state of mobile threats and defenses described in the prior sections of this report along with NCCoE's draft *Mobile Threat Catalogue*, RFI responses, and the one-on-one interviews with industry vendors. The specific state of defense is difficult to measure objectively and varies between the Android and iOS platforms based on their specific security architectures and mechanisms. The below figures are intended to provide an aggregate view.

For example, the NCCoE draft *Mobile Threat Catalogue* describes mechanisms by which malicious mobile applications can detect the presence of an application analysis environment and alter their behavior accordingly to evade detection. There are no countermeasures or only minimally effective countermeasures against such a tactic, so the box has been labeled red in Figure 22 below.

As another example described in the NCCoE *Mobile Threat Catalogue*, the application developer's compiler or other application development tools could be replaced by a malicious version that silently adds malicious code to applications. This technique was demonstrated by the XcodeGhost attack, during which a counterfeit, modified version of Apple's Xcode was distributed through a third-party website. Mitigations exist, such as downloading Xcode only from Apple's official app store (where the download process protects against modifications) or detecting unauthorized versions by having the developer manually check already-installed versions of Xcode to ensure it contains an authorized Apple signature. However, these are only partial mitigation or detection mechanisms since they depend on end-user action that is unlikely to be taken by many app developers, so the box has been labeled yellow in Figure 22.

As an example of green labeling, the techniques in the "Malicious App Delivery via Other Means" category can generally be fully mitigated or detected. Enterprise mobile devices are expected to be placed under enterprise management and management policies can be pushed to the device to prevent installation of applications from sources other than an authorized app store.

Malicious App Delivery via Official App Store	Malicious App Delivery via Other Means	Exploit via Cellular Network	Exploit via Internet	Exploit via Physical Access	Supply Chain	Exploit via Compromised Enterprise Mgmt
App analysis environment detection and evasion	Email attachment	Malicious SMS/MMS content	Malicious iOS Config Profile		Malicious compiler or other SW dev tools	Steal EMM administrator credentials
	Web site link	SMS link to malicious web content	Malicious web content	Malicious charging station		
Fake developer accounts	SMS link	Malicious update from carrier	Malicious media file	From compromised PC	Malicious or exploitable 3rd party SW libraries	Push malicious app via EMM
Stolen developer credentials	Stolen enterprise signing key	Exploit baseband radio vulnerability		Exploit unlocked or vulnerable bootloader		
Remotely install app				PIN/Password Guessing or Brute Force		Reset/remove device screen lock
Repackage or impersonate legit app				Biometric Spoofing		

Full Ability to Mitigate or Detect
Partial Ability to Mitigate or Detect
No/Minimal Ability to Mitigate or Detect

Figure 22. Defense Coverage for Pre-Device Access Tactics and Techniques

As with Figure 22, each tactic in Figure 23 and Figure 22 corresponds to one or more threats identified in this report or in the NCCoE *Mobile Threat Catalogue* and has been color-coded based on our analysis.

Persistence	Privilege Escalation	Defense Evasion	Credential Access	Discovery	Lateral Movement	Collection/Execution	Exfiltration/Cmd and Ctrl
Modify OS Kernel / Boot Partition	Exploit OS Vulnerability	Obfuscated or Encrypted Code	Credentials in Files	Application Enumeration	Exploit Cloud Services (e.g. Google Play remote app install)	Access Sensitive Data	Commonly Used Port
	Exploit TEE Vulnerability	Dynamic Code Execution	Network Sniffing	Device Type Enumeration		Lock User out of Device	Data Encrypted
Modify System Partition	Exploit Baseband Vulnerability	Disguise Root/Jailbreak Indicators	User Interface Spoofing	File and Directory Discovery	Attack PC via USB	Wipe Device Data	Multiband Communication
Modify TEE			Capture Codes sent via SMS	Local Network Configuration Discovery	Exploit enterprise servers/PCs over network	Microphone/Camera Recordings	Alternate Network Mediums (e.g. SMS, NFC, Bluetooth)
App Auto-start at Device Boot		Abuse Accessibility Features	Credentials in Device Logs	Local Network Connections Discovery		Location Tracking	
Use Android Device Admin Access to Prevent Removal			Capture Clipboard Data	Operating System Discovery		Screen and Keypress Capture	Standard App Layer Protocol
			Android Intent or iOS URL Scheme Hijacking	Process Discovery		Premium SMS Fraud	
Modify Android Cached Executable Code			Malicious Keyboard App	Security Software Discovery		Network Traffic Redirection	
						Access Contact List, Call Log, or Calendar	

Full Ability to Mitigate or Detect
Partial Ability to Mitigate or Detect
No/Minimal Ability to Mitigate or Detect

Figure 23. Defense Coverage for Post-Exploit Tactics and Techniques

General Network Based	Cellular Network Based	Device Vendor Cloud-Based	Enterprise Management Based	Physical Based
Eavesdrop on Device Comms (Voice or Data)	Downgrade to insecure protocols	Remotely track device without authorization		Obtain device backups containing sensitive data
		Remotely wipe device without authorization		Crypto side-channel attack to steal keys and decrypt data
Jamming or Denial of Service		Obtain device backups containing sensitive data	Obtain audit logs or other sensitive data	Physical eavesdropping on device use
Rogue Access Points or Base Stations (e.g. to eavesdrop or modify data or track device location)				
Modify Network Packets	Exploit SS7 to redirect calls/SMS			
Man-in-the-Middle Attacks				
	Exploit SS7 to track device location			

Full Ability to Mitigate or Detect
Partial Ability to Mitigate or Detect
No/Minimal Ability to Mitigate or Detect

Figure 24. Defense Coverage for Tactics and Techniques Without Device Access

Appendix F: Acronyms

Acronym	Definition
3GPP	Third Generation Partnership Project
5G	Fifth Generation
AES	Advanced Encryption Standard
API	Application Programming Interface
ASIC	Application-Specific Integrated Circuit
ATIS	Alliance for Telecommunications Industry Solutions
ATM	Automated Teller Machine
ATT&CK	Adversarial Tactics, Techniques, and Common Knowledge
BYOD	Bring Your Own Device
CAVP	Cryptographic Algorithm Validation Program
CC	Common Criteria
CCEVS	Common Criteria Evaluation and Validation Scheme
CCRA	Common Criteria Recognition Arrangement
CDM	Continuous Diagnostics and Mitigation
CDMA	Code Division Multiple Access
CIO	Chief Information Officer
CISO	Chief Information Security Officer
CMVP	Cryptographic Module Validation Program
CN	Core Network
CNSS	Committee on National Security Systems
COMM-ISAC	Communications Information Sharing and Analysis Center
COTS	Commercial Off-the-Shelf
CPE	Common Platform Enumeration
CPU	Central Processing Unit
CSD	Cyber Security Division
CSfC	Commercial Solutions for Classified
CSIP	Cybersecurity Strategy and Implementation Plan
CSM	Configuration Settings Management
CSRIC	Communications Security, Reliability, and Interoperability Council
CVE	Common Vulnerabilities and Exposures
CWE	Common Weakness Enumeration
DAST	Dynamic Application Security Testing
DDoS	Distributed Denial of Service
DEP	Device Enrollment Program
DGS	Digital Government Strategy
DHS	Department of Homeland Security
DoD	Department of Defense
DoS	Denial of Service
EB	Early Builder
EMM	Enterprise Mobility Management
eNodeB	Evolved Node B

Acronym	Definition
EPC	Evolved Packet Core
E-UTRAN	Evolved Universal Terrestrial Radio Access Network
FCC	Federal Communications Commission
FIPS	Federal Information Processing Standards
FISMA	Federal Information Security Modernization Act
FPGA	Field-Programmable Gate Array
FTC	Federal Trade Commission
GDP	Gross Domestic Product
GPS	Global Positioning System
GPU	Graphics Processing Unit
GSA	General Services Administration
GSM	Global System for Mobile
GSMA	Global System for Mobile Alliance
HSARPA	Homeland Security Advanced Research Projects Agency
HSS	Home Subscriber Server
HVA	High Value Assets
IA	Information Assurance
ICAMSC	Identity, Credential and Access Management Sub-Committee
IDS	Intrusion Detection System
IEEE	Institute of Electrical and Electronics Engineers
IETF	Internet Engineering Task Force
IMEI	International Mobile Equipment Identifier
IMSI	International Mobile Subscriber Identity
IoT	Internet of Things
IP	Internet Protocol
IPS	Intrusion Protection System
IPsSec	Internet Protocol Security
ISIMC	Information Security and Identity Management Committee
ISO	International Organization for Standardization
IT	Information Technology
ITL	Information Technology Laboratory
LTE	Long Term Evolution
MAM	Mobile Application Management
MAP	Mobile Application Part
MCDF	Mobile Computing Decision Framework
MDM	Mobile Device Management
MMS	Multimedia Messaging Service
MNO	Mobile Network Operator
MSRA	Mobile Security Reference Architecture
MSU	Message Signal Unit
MTTT	Mobile Technology Tiger Team
NATO	North Atlantic Treaty Organization
NCC	National Coordinating Center for Communications

Acronym	Definition
NCCIC	National Cybersecurity and Communications Integration Center
NCCoE	National Cybersecurity Center of Excellence
NFC	Near Field Communication
NG911	Next Generation 911
NIAP	National Information Assurance Partnership
NIST	National Institute of Standards and Technology
NISTIR	NIST Interagency Report
NPPD	National Protection and Programs Directorate
NPSBN	Nationwide Public Safety Broadband Network
NSA	National Security Agency
NSC	National Security Council
NSS	National Security Systems
NVD	National Vulnerability Database
OCISO	Office of the Chief Information Security Officer
OEM	Original Equipment Manufacturer
OMB	Office of Management and Budget
OS	Operating System
OSS	Operational Support System
OTT	Over-The-Top
OWASP	Open Web Application Security Project
PC	Personal Computer
PCL	Product Compliant List
PCRF	Policy and Charging Rules Function
PII	Personally Identifiable Information
PIN	Personal Identification Number
PIV	Personal Identity Verification
PIV-I	PIV-Interoperability
PKI	Public Key Infrastructure
PP	Protection Profile
PSAP	Public Safety Answering Point
PSTN	Public Switched Telephone Network
R&D	Research and Development
RAM	Random-Access Memory
RAN	Radio Access Network
RF	Radio Frequency
RFI	Request for Information
RFP	Request for Proposal
RIFS	Roaming and Interconnect Fraud and Security
RKP	Real-time Kernel Protection
ROM	Read-Only Memory
S&T	Science and Technology
SAE	System Architecture Evolution
SCTP	Stream Control Transmission Protocol

Acronym	Definition
SD	Secure Digital
SDK	Software Development Kit
SDO	Standards Development Organizations
SDR	Software Defined Radio
SELinux	Security Enhanced Linux
SIEM	Security Information and Event Management
SIG	Bluetooth Special Interest Group
SIM	Subscriber Identity Module
SMS	Short Message Service
SP	Special Publication
SS7	Signaling System 7
SSL	Secure Sockets Layer
SSO	Single Sign-On
STIX	Structured Threat Information eXpression
STP	Signaling Transfer Point
TAXII	Trusted Automated eXchange of Indicator Information
TCG	Trusted Computing Group
TEE	Trusted Execution Environment
TIC	Trusted Internet Connection
TIMA	TrustZone-based Integrity Measurement Architecture
TLS	Transport Layer Security
TPM	Trusted Platform Module
UAE	United Arab Emirates
UE	User Equipment
UICC	Universal Integrated Circuit Card
UMTS	Universal Mobile Telecommunications System
USB	Universal Serial Bus
USB-IF	USB Implementers Forum
US-CERT	United States Computer Emergency Readiness Team
USIM	Universal Subscriber Identity Module
VoIP	Voice over IP
VPN	Virtual Private Network
VTS	Vulnerability Test Suite
VUL	Vulnerability Management
WPA	Wi-Fi Protected Access
WPS	Wi-Fi Protected Setup

www.ingramcontent.com/pod-product-compliance
Lightning Source LLC
Chambersburg PA
CBHW041419050326
40689CB00002B/568